Ghost Stories of Sarasota

Ghost Stories

of

Sarasota

Kim Cool

HISTORIC VENICE PRESS

Also by Kim Cool:
Ghost Stories of Venice

Ghost Stories of Sarasota

Historic Venice Press, P. O. Box 800, Venice, FL 34284

941.468-6556

kimcool@www.historicvenicepress.com

First Edition 2003
Printed in the United States of America
ISBN   0-9721655-1-7

Dedication

With the publication of *Ghost Stories of Venice*, I realized that the picturesque if circuitous path I had followed in my life had suddenly taken yet another turn, the most interesting turn of all. I was living a charmed life, signing books, giving talks, meeting more interesting and enchanting people with each day that passed — all because of a chance meeting with another writer from another place, many miles from my adopted hometown of Venice, Florida. It was that other writer who suggested I write that first book of ghost stories. It is that other writer who continues to offer advice and encouragement.

My father told me my first ghost stories.

My daughter listened to the stories I made up for her when she was young.

My husband cheered on my artistic adventures.

My friend and colleague guided me the rest of the way.

This book is for all four of you: Herman Patmore, Heidi Adams Cool, Kenneth Adams Cool Jr. and Charles J. Adams III.

Thanks for being there for me.

Contents

1 THEATRICAL GHOSTS ... 1

The Players Theatre ... 3

Florida Studio Theatre ... 9

Theatre Works ... 13

The Golden Apple Dinner Theatre ... 18

The Asolo Theatre Company ... 34

The Sarasota Opera House ... 43

2 SINGULAR SPIRITS ... 48

Probable cause ... 50

Visiting ghost ... 55

The Pelican Man's dovecote ... 59

3 NEIGHBORHOODS ... 63

Indian Beach ... 64

Holmes Beach ... 67

Little in common ... 71

Where there's smoke ... 78

Towles Court for art's sake ... 80

Lido Key ... 86

4 INDIAN SPIRITS ... 92

Three little Indians ... 93

5 CIRCUS GHOSTS ... 97

Dusty's best friend ... 98

6 EDUCATIONAL GHOSTS ... 105

Haunting prepper ... 106

In the still of the night ... 108

New College, old ghost ... 118

All stirred up ... 121

7 GRAVEYARD SHIFT ... 129

Graven images ... 130

8 RINGLINGS & FRIENDS ... 132

Home again to Ca d'Zan ... 133

Ringlings' last hurrah ... 143

Behind the locked gate ... 157

Ca d'Zan beckons ... 167

Beyond the crypt ... 170

About the author ... 173

Ackowledgments ... 174

Bibliography ... 175

Order form... 177

Afterword ... 178

Introduction

As I began to research *Ghost Stories of Sarasota*, my second book relating to things that go bump in the night along the Gulf Coast of Florida, I discovered an eerie connection with *Ghost Stories of Venice*.

The characters involved in the first story penned, "Don't Call Me Madame," were actors encountered by me during my early years as a reporter for the *Venice Gondolier Sun*. Also involved was a youthful drunk driver now serving time in prison for his part in the circumstances that led to the story. The tale was told to me by the Players' actor who experienced the spooky event in the dimly lit theater. It played out during a rehearsal for another show.

Other stories were tied to Venice only because they involved similar occurrences. A story about a mystery lady and a copy machine that churns out multiple sheets of paper after hours and even when turned off, is somewhat similar to the tale of the cowboy ghost in a Venice office park. He too works only late at night.

Then there were stories that were unique to Sarasota, the older of the two cities.

Venice celebrated its 75th birthday in 2000. Sarasota celebrated its 100th birthday the following year.

Venice is a planned community, tracing its history and development to homesteaders, wealthy Chicago

Kim Cool

widow Bertha Palmer and to the Brotherhood of
Locomotive Engineers and city planner John Nolen.

While Palmer was a major landowner in Sarasota
County, the city of Sarasota owes more to its Scottish
heritage and to John and Charles Ringling of the circus
family. And, while city planners have appeared from
time to time to place their stamp on the city, no one person or group ever planned the entire city to the degree
that Nolen planned Venice.

Instead it almost seems as though there was some
sort of magnetic force field that drew certain people to
Sarasota at a time when many of their friends were
profiting handsomely on the East Coast of the state.

No other city in Florida has earned such a strong
reputation for its residents' support of the arts, nor has
any other Florida City ever been such a magnet for people in the arts as well as people who appreciate the arts.

Several people with whom I spoke think there is a
mystical quality about the area. They spoke of the white
sugar sand of Siesta Key's beach, saying it was pulver-
ized crystals and thus imbued with mystical powers.
One lady spoke of the important religious rituals conducted by Native Americans long ago on the same site
where the Towles Court Artist Colony is located today.

Whether lured by magic crystals, benevolent spirits
or other means, Sarasota residents and visitors are more

likely to be writers or artists.

The director of the Sarasota County Arts Council credits the development of the arts in Sarasota directly to real estate developer and circus owner John Ringling, founder of the John & Mable Ringling Museum of Art.

Ringling's museum was established as a hook to set Sarasota apart from other Florida cities during the land boom of the 1920s. From that museum grew the Asolo Theatre Company, the Sarasota Ballet and the Sarasota Opera.

Whenever the initial cultural seed was planted, it was certainly well tended by the Ringlings and all those who have followed them to Sarasota.

As I learned on Feb. 4, 2003, the spirits of many of the people who followed the Ringlings to Sarasota, are still there.

Thanks to Rev. Pat Charnley of the Angel Ministries in Venice and Carole Lee, a medium for the Angel Ministries, Ron McCarty who is known as The Keeper of Ca d'Zan (the John and Mable Ringling mansion), a local TV crew and I were able to connect with the spirits of John and Mable and literally hundreds of their late friends, associates, neighbors and assorted circus performers during a special event at the historic and newly renovated and restored home on that very special evening.

The two lengthiest tales in this book grew out of that

private after-hours visit to Ca d'Zan.

People with an affinity for the arts have continued to come to Sarasota, even during the city's lean years when the Florida land boom went bust and the Great Depression cast its dark shadows over the whole United States. To this day, the arts remain the city's most powerful lure, even more so than its sugar sand beaches and magical sunsets.

Those people have continued to expand Ringling's vision even as the area from Sarasota to Venice has become known as the Cultural Coast.

Perhaps that is why its spirit and its spirits are different from those of other Florida cities.

There may be ghosts along Sarasota's beaches, but the most interesting specters were discovered right where they were expected to be — in the theatres, the museums, the historic homes and on the sites of sacred Indian lands.

While most West Coast Florida spirits seem to be younger than their East Coast Florida counterparts, a few ancient Indian spirits have continued to watch over their ancestral homes for more than 1,000 years. There also are a few pirate ghosts along the shores of the Gulf of Mexico and some of those are nearly as old as the ghosts of the Spanish explorers who have haunted St. Augustine, the oldest city in America, since the 16th century.

Ghost hunting in Sarasota has been decidedly easier than ghost hunting in the much smaller city of Venice. Yet tracking down these spirits would not have been possible without the help of a number of people, especially Rev. Pat Charnley, Carol Lee, Cathleen Carillo, Anne Cederberg, Rilla Fleming, Kelly Fores, Carol Harwood, Jeanne Lambert, Kim Noah, Debbie Perez, Ron McCarty and so many others.

As I continue to "go haunting," I continue to be grateful for the help and inspiration I have received from my friend and colleague, Charles J. Adams III, one of America's most prolific authors of ghost stories.

Watch out St. Petersburg and Tampa, the ghost lady is coming your way next.

Kim Cool
Venice, Florida
June 2003

Kim Cool

Part I

Theatrical Ghosts

Kim Cool

Don't "Call me Madame"

All one has to do is ask.

People do not go out of their way to relate their experiences with ghosts, specters, wraiths, poltergeists and other things that go bump in the night.

Yet, when coming in contact with one who would be receptive to a ghost story, most people willingly share their experiences. That was the case at The Players Theatre in Sarasota where I uncovered the Don't "Call Me Madame" tale.

3

Kim Cool

I had just finished touring the theater with its executive director, Burton Wolfe, when I asked if there were any ghost stories connected with the building which houses the city's oldest community theater.

Wolfe said he thought that one of his stage managers, Patty Atkins, might know a tale or two.

It turned out he was right.

Photo by Kim Cool

The ghost of a talented young actress who was killed in a tragic accident has been seen back stage at The Players Theatre in Sarasota. The Players is the oldest theater in the heart of the Cultural Coast.

Atkins knew a very good tale indeed, one in which her husband had been an active participant.

It turned out that the 70-year-old theater — the oldest theater in Sarasota — had recently become the home of one of the city's newest and youngest ghosts.

As this story unfolded backstage at that venerable old theater, it seems appropriate to set the scene and introduce these players at The Players.

The characters are a young actress, her actor boyfriend, the stage manager and the stage manager's husband Robert , also a Players actor, and a 16-year old drunk driver.

Just 16 when she crossed to the other side, the young actress, Lauren Melville, also may be the most beautiful and talented spectre on the theater's other stage.

Melville died tragically on Dec. 27, 1997, the victim of a freak car accident that was set in motion by a drunk driver named Mark Chapman, also 16 at the time.

Just a few weeks earlier, she had been garnering rave reviews for her role as the female lead in "How To Succeed In Business Without Really Trying," opposite Joe Spieldenner, at the Venice Little Theatre.

Seemingly destined for stardom, Melville was celebrating at a party in her hometown of Sarasota. She was sitting on the lawn with three friends when the sorry chain of events that caused her death began .

Chapman, with a blood alcohol level of .06, drove his Mustang into a Mitsubishi, pushing that car into another car. That car was propelled some 40 feet, killing Melville instantly, and seriously injuring the three friends who were life-flighted to Bayfront Medical Center in Tampa.

Melville's boyfriend, Steve Dawson, also a local actor, had been cast in "Call Me Madame," the January 1998 main stage offering at The Players.

Unsuspectingly cast in the role of the narrator for this particular ghost story was Robert Atkins, another actor at The Players. He is married to Patty. He also had been cast in "Call Me Madame." It was one of his first roles at The Players.

On the night when this particular story unfolded, Atkins and Patty had arrived about a half hour before one of the rehearsals for "Call Me Madame." Patty was assistant stage manager of the production.

Atkins said that he was back stage when he noticed a young girl at stage right, the area where the paint room and costume area were located.

"As an ex-cop I am always security conscious," he said. "We had a lot of homeless people camping out in the woods behind The Players then.

"My concern was that someone would be back there to steal something. The homeless would come in to steal clothes or makeup or wallets. She didn't seem to have any purpose but she seemed too young to be a homeless person."

Atkins said that he left to do something and when he returned the young girl was at stage left.

"I asked her if I could help her and she said 'No'," he said. "It was dark there then. There was no blue lighting like we have now, and the back side of the stage was dark."

He was on the side with the dressing rooms and after watching her for about 10 minutes, he did not pay any more attention to her he said.

"A week later I was in the men's dressing room and Steve had this picture in the mirror," Atkins said. "I went by it the first time but then I said to him, 'Is that your girlfriend? She was in the theater last week.' He turned white."

But then the director called everyone to the stage, the rehearsal began and there was no more time to discuss Dawson's reaction.

It wasn't until the following week that Atkins learned about the accident.

"She was probably looking for him (Steve Dawson),"

Atkins said. "Steve said he had felt some strange things but didn't put much stock in it at the time."

Atkins said he had no doubt that he had seen Melville because of her infectious smile. The girl in Dawson's photograph and the girl that Atkins saw backstage both had the same smile.

"We always got there early, about a half hour before the rest of the cast would arrive," he said. "That is why she stood out. There was hardly anyone else there. She was there for a period of time and there was no mistaking that smile."

Atkins said he had never seen a ghost before, had never even thought much about ghosts. He has not seen one since then but his outlook has changed.

"Steve was in shock, but I know who I saw."

The following April, Chapman was found guilty of DUI manslaughter and was sentenced to prison for 15 years. That sentence was later reduced to 10.75 years.

Dawson's career has continued to blossom on the Sarasota theatrical front and Atkins has begun to develop a following at local comedy clubs.

There have been no more reported sightings of Melville.

No ghosts in "site"

Built in 1915 for the Sarasota Woman's Club, the home of the Florida Studio Theatre (FST) main stage (The Keating Theatre) is in the oldest building used by any of the city's acting companies.

That alone should have guaranteed a ghost or two but whenever I asked any of its employees the response I got was beginning to sound like the party line — "there are no ghosts here."

Refusing to believe that FST was ghostless, I kept up my barrage of questions, finally going right to the top, to

Kim Cool

Photo by Kim Cool

The walls of the Florida Studio Theatre reverberated with
rapping, tapping and so many unpleasant occurrences
that the artistic directors hired exorcists to cleanse the old
building so the show(s) could go on.

Ghost Stories of Sarasota

FST's executive artistic director, Richard Hopkins.

At the Venice Little Theatre, I had found nothing but a ghost light and a few stories of strange noises. In Sarasota, it seemed as though every single theater was haunted by at least one spirit with one possible exception — The Florida Studio Theatre, despite its historic home.

The old building had nearly been razed to become a parking lot when it was saved by Joe and Marian McKenna for FST. They bought the land and the old clubhouse in 1982 for $100,000 and leased it rent-free to the theatrical company.

"It was where she got her first kiss," Hopkins said of Marian McKenna who had a soft spot in her heart for the old clubhouse turned theater.

If the site had been the site of both real and imagined passion all those years, it would seem that at least one spirit might have remained. Just one Thespian spook was all I asked.

As it turned out, Hopkins gave me far more.

"In 1980 when I first came to the theater, I would not work in the theater by myself," he said. "There were a great many spirits there and they were not nice ones.

"We were having many instances each day. There were rappings on the walls, tappings in the theater, falling objects and all sorts of other mysterious occurrences."

Hopkins was not the only one who did not want to be in the theater alone. A buddy system was adopted in those early days so that no one was ever by himself in any part of the building, especially late at night when it was time to lock up after the final rehearsals. It got so bad that Hopkins and his associate, Kate Alexander, decided to take matters into their own hands.

"We used our own money to hire a priest to cleanse the building," he said. "They found some very nasty things there. They had to come back twice and it took five years before things were better. We're fine now."

In those early days, there were spaces in the building that were unused, Hopkins said. It was in those places that the priests found the largest assortment of evil spirits.

"They (two women) cleared the building for 24 hours," he said. "It took them about two-three hours each time. They brought candles, incense and bells."

Hopkins said he could not remember the names of the two women who accomplished the cleansing but that finally, the theatrical company had the building all to itself. Or maybe the spirits had become friendlier.

All in a day's haunting

While gathering ghost stories, I have learned to expect the unexpected.

But this coincidence (or whatever it was) did surprise me a bit.

It was a Tuesday morning when I got a phone call from Michael Marcello, the managing artistic director of Theatre Works in Sarasota. He finally had the time to tell me about that theater's ghost, "Warm and Fuzzy."

That is a strange name for something that is more often thought to send chills up one's spine or even to cause a chilly breeze to waft through an area but Marcello said his theater's ghost is different.

"Our ghost is quite congenial," he said. "There is nothing threatening about the ghost at Theatre Works.

"He doesn't really have a name but we all refer to him as 'Warm and Fuzzy' because that is how he makes us feel in the theater.

"Whenever we enter the building we feel his presence. No matter where we go, we feel like he is going ahead of us, sweeping the floor and paving our way, making it nicer.

"It is like that when we leave the dressing room and go on stage. He is always there, going ahead of us and looking out for us."

Marcello went on to say that he thinks the warm and fuzzy ghost has been at the theater since its very earliest days.

"The ghost is probably left over from the days when this building housed the Palm Tree Playhouse," he said.

That would make this specter nearly 80 years old.

The Palm Tree Playhouse occupied the building at 1247 First St. in the 1920s and 1930s. It was the first theater in Sarasota. Then it was a movie theater for several years and later hosted the old Siesta Key Players and even the Asolo II Theatre Company before falling into severe disrepair and sitting empty (except for its ghost) for some years.

In 1984, a group of actors who had met while performing at the Venice Little Theater, decided they could not bear to part. Led by Jack Taylor who provided the start-up money, they combined their elbow grease and enthusiasm and formed Theatre Works, giving the old ghost a new home in the process.

From the first season, the winter of 1985-86, Theatre Works Thespians had performed musicals, dramas, comedies and musical reviews, employing professionals for the most part. One of its biggest successes in recent

Photo by Kim Cool

At Sarasota's Theatre Works a character known for sending chills up and down one's spine is known by the name of "Warm and Fuzzy."

15

years was bringing Marcello into the troupe as the
director of "Bravo Caruso," a tale about the late tenor.
That production was performed at Theatre Works in
2001.

Five days before opening night, Marcello's talents
were sorely tested.

The man playing the lead role of Caruso became ill.

There was no understudy but, as the director,
Marcello knew the part fairly well and, fortuitously —
he can sing. In true show must go on fashion, Marcello
took on the role. Script in hand and with a warm and
fuzzy ghost at his side, Marcello appeared on stage,
garbed as the late singer. Bearing a strong resemblance
to Caruso, Marcello earned rave reviews from critics
and audiences alike. Less than a year later, in 2002,
Marcello was put in charge of the theater.

Did something intervene to bring this about?

No one can be certain but something had drawn
Marcello to spend more time at the theater.

Although he continued to perform, as the managing
director, he found that he had a nearly round-the-clock
job selecting scripts, securing directors, casts, money
and all the things needed to keep the theater going.

What he has not found was the ghost although
Marcello said that he knew the warm and fuzzy spirit

was there.

"You never feel alone in the theater," he said. "That ghost has been there as long as I can remember."

Two hours after Marcello made that statement to me, Julie, a waitress at the Venice Yacht Club gave me a different slant on the Theatre Works ghost. Was this a coincidence, or not? I was at the club for a presentation of "Ghost Stories of Venice." When through with that talk I casually mentioned the Theatre Works ghost story which I had just learned. Julie overheard me. She shared her experiences as a young girl in the old Palm Tree Playhouse, which had been located in the same space.

"I remember him," Julie said. "Everyone was afraid of him even though we never actually saw him. A bunch of us took drama classes at the Palm Tree Playhouse when we were little. We all knew about that ghost."

She said that though they never saw him they sometimes heard him. Certain that he was not a warm and fuzzy specter, they never went to the theater by themselves and they made sure they were never alone anywhere in the building. The building is not large as theaters go, having just a 30-foot stage but it does have its nooks and crannies, small dressing rooms, places to store the scenery and more than enough room for a ghost.

Some folks mellow with age.

Perhaps the same thing happens to ghosts.

Kim Cool

"She" takes care of them

Since 1970, the Golden Apple Dinner Theatre has been offering "Broadway on the Suncoast."

The longest-running dinner theater in Florida is known for its musical shows as well as its meal service.

It has not been so well known for its ghosts although it seems to have enough for a spirited repertory troupe according to theater owner Roberta McDonald, her daughter Kyle Ennis Turoff, son Ben and long time employee, Donna Des Isles. Des Isles has been with the Turoffs for 30 years as of 2003. Each has experienced one

18

or more of these energetic entities at one or more times during the past several years. Some of the specters have made repeated curtain calls and show no sign of taking their show(s) on the road.

That is very much in keeping with the spirit of the Golden Apple, a unique operation in the annals of community theater. The company's origins are entwined completely with a love story as charming as any that has been produced by the company. And with more than 300 productions staged, that is saying something.

McDonald, the first female star of the Today Show on NBC-TV, was just about to make it big on Broadway when she met Robert Ennis Turoff and the two fell in love.

It is a classic American love story that would make for an excellent theatrical production itself.

Turning her back on TV stardom and a promising Broadway career, she married Turoff and together, they opened their first theater in an old supermarket in Sarasota.

Two children, Ben and Kyle, followed in their parents footsteps and now, more than 40 years later, the Turoff family is considered the Suncoast's one true theatrical dynasty. The original Apple was the longest running dinner theater in the country as of 2003, when a documentary was filmed about its history, long-term employees and players. The four Turoffs manage the original Golden Apple Dinner Theatre in Sarasota and the newer Venice Golden Apple Dinner Theatre, housed in the Holiday Inn of Venice. They own a third theater in St. Petersburg and annually produce at least one show in Singapore.

What they do not manage are the ghosts.

McDonald told me about three of them. She knows the history of two of the ghosts and how their stories are tied to the history of the two-story Golden Apple building. The site has not always been a theater.

Once, long ago there was a car dealership on the property at 25 Pineapple Ave., home of the Sarasota Golden Apple Dinner Theatre. McDonald said she thinks that the car dealership may have been the home of the theater's one four-legged ghost, an Irish Setter. The dog might have been a watchdog for the car dealership but this is only a guess on her part.

Des Isles had an entirely different take on the four-legged vision, calling it a possible example of precognition.

"I saw the dog," she said. "I saw it four times and then once more eight years later."

The first four times she saw the dog, she was alone in the theater late at night. Des Isles waits tables at the

Photo by Kim Cool

The Golden Apple Dinner Theatre offers "Broadway on the Suncoast" and a variety of spirits, both liquid and ethereal, to its patrons.

theater but she also works as a theater techie, painting sets and doing other behind-the-scenes jobs as needed.

She was painting the floor of the stage late one night. They always paint the stage just before or just after the opening of a show and it needs to be done late at night after everyone has gone so that no one will walk on it while the paint is still wet, she said.

"I saw a tail swish by," she said. "It was an Irish Setter. It didn't come to bother me so I just kept painting.

"I didn't pay any more attention but decided that someone must have been in the theater with their dog.

"But there was no one else in the building and then the dog just disappeared. I didn't see him disappear but he wasn't there anymore."

While he had been there, she saw him run along the lower tier of tables toward the back of the theater and across the back. The dog would stop at each corner, panting and looking right at her.

The Golden Apple Theatre in Sarasota has two tiers of tables and chairs in a U-shape around a lower level filled with additional tables and chairs in front of the stage.

Des Isles said the dog appeared on three more occasions, always doing exactly the same thing, and never bothering her work. Each time, she checked to see if its owner was in the theater and each time she realized that she was alone in the building. Each time she told Bob Turoff about the dog the next day and each time, he told her she was probably over-tired, she said. Then, she did not see the dog for quite some time.

"Eight years later, it happened again," she said. "It did exactly what I had seen it do."

But this time, neither she nor the dog were alone.

The dog, named Flambeau, was accompanied by its owner, David Ferguson. Bob Turoff and some other Apple employees also were in the theater.

This time, the dog went right up on the stage with Des Isles.

She was so excited that she told everyone that this was the dog she had seen so often in the past. The mystery was solved.

Or maybe not.

Ferguson had the last word.

"I've never brought him here before," he said.

Was this a case of precognition or was Flambeau a twin of the theater's four-legged ghost?

Flambeau has since passed on to the other side so if the Irish setter makes another appearance, precognition can probably be ruled out.

Kim Cool

Photo by Kim Cool
**Kyle Ennis Turoff
with a fan like the
one that fell from
the wig shelf
onto a performer.**

Roberta has no doubts about the two female ghosts
that she has seen, nor does Kyle have any doubts about
a male spirit she saw during a performance in what
appears to be the most haunted theater in Sarasota.

The first ghost most certainly dates to the days when
there was a Morrison's Cafeteria on the site. There were
hundreds of Morrison cafeterias all over Florida until

the late 1990s. The one on this particular site closed in the late 1960s, shortly before the opening of the theater. There was a theater nearby but that one, formerly the old Edwards Theater, at 61 Pineapple Ave., was destined to become the home of the Sarasota Opera, one of just seven opera houses in the United States to be owned by its opera company.

The future home of the Golden Apple, at 25 Pineapple Ave., would need some extensive renovations before it would become a dinner theater.

When owned by Morrisons, the two-story building housed a cafeteria on the main floor and rest rooms for the help, offices and a play room for the employee's children on the second floor.

Segregation was still prevalent throughout the south, necessitating separate facilities for blacks and whites as well as for men and women.

"Where the dressing rooms are now, was the place where the kids stayed," Kyle said.

The ghost in question was a black lady, employed to care for the children of Morrison employees.

"I have seen her," McDonald said. "She looks just like Aunt Jemima, with the head scarf and all."

When asked if her husband had also seen her she replied that one "must believe in order to see a ghost."

Kim Cool

Photo by Kim Cool

Director Robert Ennis Turoff (seated on left in dark sweater) is the only member of the Golden Apple's founding family who has not seen an Apple ghost. Nor did he see the orbs that appeared in this photo that was taken during a rehearsal of the 2003 production of "Damn Yankees."

Robert, the Apple's producer and a highly regarded director, is the one member of the family who has not experienced a ghost at the theater — yet.

That much was clear to me even before I finished my first collection of ghostly tales. Those who are open to the idea of ghosts are much more likely to see an occasional wisp of something or even a whole being.

Of course, in the case of the Golden Apple, it could be that these shadowy actors are themselves spooked about appearing before the revered director.

The Golden Apple's "Mammy" has been around for years, MacDonald said.

The Mammy watches over the theater and its many musical productions as she once watched over the children so many years earlier.

"She protects our staff," Kyle said. "Terry protects our staff too and she even leaves us presents."

Terry is one of two former actors who have yet to make their final curtain call at the theater. Her last name was Pyrenne. Her father was the musical director of the circus before his retirement.

Pyrenne's ghost has been seen several times by MacDonald. The actress was just 27 or 28 when she died of collapsed lungs caused by a major asthma attack, Kyle said.

"She is always leaving presents on people's tables," Kyle said, "she leaves a wishbone, or moves some eyelashes, nothing major.

"She was very outspoken about who she liked. She could make life a living hell."

According to Kyle, she continued her ways after her death, once causing a small fan to fly off a shelf in the women's dressing room and hit a stage manager in the head.

Pyrenne had acted in many shows at the Golden

Kim Cool

Apple, including the Apple's first production of "Fiddler on the Roof." She directed "By Strauss" and "The Fantastiks."

The date of Pyrenne's death was Dec. 10, 1988.

The fourth spirit, actor Bud Welters, died more recently — in 1996.

His ghost was seen first by Kyle but also by another Apple performer..

For many years he was a service station attendant at the Texaco Station at U.S. 41 and Hillview and whenever Bob Turoff would stop there to buy gasoline, Welters would say that he wanted to act at the Golden Apple. Turoff told him to come to an audition and he finally did, eventually acting in about eight or 10 productions, Kyle said.

"He had the time of his life here," she said. "He was here for several years. He died very suddenly."

The next year, Kyle was appearing in "The Unsinkable Molly Brown."

"It was a Saturday night, the top of the act and I (Molly) was talking about Colorado and when I looked out I saw Bud at the top of the stairs," Kyle said. "I must have read my lines differently because when I came off the stage, my friend Charlene who was helping me change costumes, asked me what happened and

Sun photo by Kim Cool

The orbs in this photo were captured on film during a
rehearsal of "Damn Yankee' at the Sarasota Golden Apple
Dinner Theatre. They appeared in just one other photo
taken that day.

29

Kim Cool

why I had changed my lines.

"Charlene was living with musical director Michael Sebastian and his companion at the time. The next day she mentioned the incident to Michael."

It turned out that Sebastian had seen him too.

"Michael said, 'When I turned around toward the drummer, Bud was on the steps behind the drummer in the pit.' "

There's more.

It seems that Kyle's husband overheard her telling me about having seen Welters.

Two days later, Kyle told me the rest of the story.

"My husband asked me if Bud was a big guy," she said. "Then he said that during the last couple of strikes (taking the set down), he had seen something or someone that looked like him.

"And Ben (Kyle's brother) saw him too."

There also is a specter at the Golden Apple that no one has seen.

This may be a case of hearing is believing.

Both Kyle and Donna have heard a piano playing when no one is around to play it.

"I have heard the pianist," Donna said. "But I have never seen him."

One night, Donna and set designer Ray Perry were

30

in the theater, painting the floor for another show. They both heard piano music but paid little attention.

Frequently, at that hour, there might be a pianist there, working on adapting the book for the five-eight musicians in the orchestra, Donna said.

"Then I realized that it wasn't the music from the show coming up," she said, "and I wanted to know who was up there."

At the theater, the musicians are in a booth to the right of the stage. One door offers the only easy access although it would be possible to jump down through the opening that faces the audience. Usually that opening is covered by a scrim and often by heavy curtains. The night in question, the curtains were drawn so it was impossible to see if anyone was in the booth. Yet the two painters had no doubt that the music was coming from the booth. Donna decided to go see who was in the booth, leaving Ray on the stage.

"I called out, 'Who is playing?' but no one answered," she said. "I went into the booth through the door and there was no one there.

"When I got back to the stage I asked Ray if he saw who jumped down from the music booth. 'No one' he said. It was really cool, good music, but no one saw anyone."

Kim Cool

Unless the piano player was a woman.

For Donna had yet another ghost story to relate.

"There used to be a large curved mirror up in the grid near the stage manager's booth," she said. "The stage manager could see all the action in that curved screen.

"Kay Daffney's husband was appearing in the 'Lion in Winter,' and he was on the stairs over there (she pointed to stage right) and he saw a woman's face in the mirror," Donna continued. "Full face."

The Golden Apple Dinner Theatre may not be the oldest theater in town but it certainly appears to be the most haunted.

If nothing else, it gives new meaning to the term "extras" when it comes to actors.

The Apple also is unique for the camaraderie of its staff, many of whom have been around as long as DesIsles. Even the chef has been there for 23 years and one of the newest waiters for 21 years.

Those involved are like one large family. Perhaps that is why Pyrenne and Welters have both decided to extend their runs in this particular theater.

Or, it may be, that they have other aspirations for the Sarasota Opera House is right next door.

Sometime after this story was "finished," I learned

32

that there could be one or more other spirited specters at the Golden Apple — the phantoms of the Opera House.

According to Chris Burtless, the building engineer of the Sarasota Opera House complex, there is a being that seems to haunt the Peterson Great Room in his building and there seems to be another specter that goes back and forth between the Apple building and the opera house complex, an entity in search of a friend, a long-lost friend. There will be more about this in the chapter referring to the Sarasota Opera House.

Kim Cool

Sarasota's immigrant ghost

For more than 40 years, the Asolo Theatre Company has been an important part of the professional theatrical scene in Sarasota.

The theater company housed there is an important link in the chain of arts organizations that developed over the years in Sarasota. Its ghost has an even lengthier pedigree.

Unlike other theatrical specters that have adopted their individual theatrical homes, the Asolo ghost is thought to have arrived with the theater.

The company's first home was the 18th century

Asolo Theatre in Asolo, Italy.

The lovely old Italian building had opened there in 1798, was refurbished in 1857, demolished in 1929, and consigned to a warehouse until it was purchased by the estate of John Ringling in 1949.

It was reconstructed within one of the galleries of the John and Mable Ringling Museum of Art. In 1957 it was moved into its own specially designed theater building, eventually becoming the home of the Asolo Opera Company and a summer theater company.

Photo by Kim Cool

A Scottish ghost is said to haunt the upper balcony of the Mertz Theatre used by the Asolo Theatre Festival in Sarasota.

Kim Cool

By 1966, the professional company had become known as the Asolo Theatre Festival and was operating year-round.

Despite the historic building and restoration work that certainly should have awakened some of the dead, the Asolo seemed to have remained ghostless.

At about the same time, an alliance was formed with the Florida State University School of Theatre. By 1973 the university shifted its entire actor training program from Tallahassee to Sarasota, giving birth to the FSU/Asolo Conservatory for Actor Training.

The two theatrical companies managed to coexist and grow year by year until 1990 when they finally were able to move into newer quarters within a new building, designed for their special needs.

A year earlier, the opera had also acquired a new home when the old Edwards Theatre underwent its third incarnation, to become the home of the Sarasota Opera.

The two acting companies were joined by a third party, a being from Dunfermline, Scotland, that had somehow survived the long distance move. It was sort of a package deal, a ghost and a theater, all in a box.

The charming old Italian theater which had provid-ed the acting company with its name was assigned a gentler role, housing meetings and lectures rather than full-blown theatrical productions.

Named the FSU Center, by 1994 the new building had two theaters, costume and prop shops, many offices, a green room and an exercise room for the actors.

The smaller 161-seat Jane B. Cook Theatre was built to showcase smaller productions and has become the space in which the conservatory students perform.

The larger of the two theaters became the destination of the gilded and ghostlier "theater in a box," the circa 1903 Dunfermline Opera House.

Like the old Asolo theater, the opera house had been taken down and boxed before being sold to the theatrical company in Sarasota.

With an expanded proscenium opening, the old opera house was installed within the 500-seat Harold E. and Esther M. Mertz Theatre in the new FSU Center, eventually becoming home to the Asolo Theatre Company's main stage productions.

The story of the reconstructed theater's ghost came from the historian of the old opera house, Gerry McMullan, of Dunfermline.

In 2002, in celebration of the 100th anniversary of the city of Sarasota, negotiations were undertaken to join Sarasota and Dunfermline as Sister Cities. Shortly after

returning to Scotland, McMullan, one of the Dunfermline delegates, shared his story of the old opera house.

"This may not be a ghost story," he wrote. "I can
only leave that up to you to decide."

McMullan said that just prior to the demolition of
the old opera house in the early 1980s, he received per-
mission to enter the aged building with a select group of
people who were interested in the old edifice. His plan
was to take pictures.

"I was standing in the upper balcony with Mr. Bell,
who at that time used the theater as an upholstery
workshop," McMullan said. "I inquired if there were
any seats left in the building, to which he replied there
were none. They had all been destroyed, he said.

"At this point he left me alone to carry on with my work."

McMullan continued that after a few moments, he
noticed an old heavy door behind an old security safe.

"Curiosity got the better of me and I decided to try
to move the safe and see what lay behind the door," he
said. "At this point all my friends were downstairs so I
slowly moved the old safe and had to really push back
the door with a great deal of effort."

The door had been closed for some 35 years, he said.
It took all his strength to pry it open. When it was fully
open and his eyes had adjusted to the dark light in the

Photo by Kim Cool
Gerry McMullan, archivist of the Dunfermline Opera House, formerly located in Dunfermline, Scotland, is shown in the old theater's balcony, now serving the Asolo Theatre Festival in Sarasota.

space, he made a startling discovery. Lying before him, dismantled and ready to move out, were all the seats that had been located in the opera house balcony.

"After all these years I finally found seating which everyone had assumed was lost forever," he said.

McMullan said that he was not brave enough to enter the attic at that point, so he retreated to the balcony and resumed his picture taking.

"Now for the scary part," he said. "There was no draft or wind in the building but I heard what can only be described as a loud sigh coming from the attic.

"As I turned to see who was behind me, the old metal door suddenly slammed shut and the whole building seemed to shake with the noise.

"You can imagine that I was taking the stairs three at

a time and when I got to the bottom and said what happened, no one had heard a thing. I did not see anyone and the door was well and truly open and could not possibly slam as hard as it did without any help."

As I discovered in talking to people for my first book of ghost stories, sometimes there is no visible proof of what happened. Spirits appear in all manner of ways. In "Ghost Stories of Venice," there were more tales of unexplained phenomena such as this door slamming incident than there were of actual sightings of three-dimensional figures.

That could be a Southwest Florida phenomenon but I think not.

There seem to be nearly as many ways for spirits to make themselves known as there are people who are likely to experience the specters' various paranormal escapades.

Some people see three-dimensional beings. On occasion, they might even have a brief conversation with a ghost.

Others see only shadowy shapes, nearly always either blue or white (at least in Venice, Fla.), while many simply hear sounds like moving furniture or loud sighs such as the sound experienced by McMullan. Still others may experience an odor, a flash of light or running water from a faucet that somehow turns itself on for no apparent reason.

That door that slammed shut in Dunfermline all those years ago is in the reconstructed theater in Sarasota.

"This is where the door led up to the attic," McMullan said in April 2003 when he was again in Sarasota. After meeting for lunch, we went up into the very top rows of the balcony where McMullan pointed to the spot where he had stood when he experienced the ghost.

If you are of a mind, take one of the theater tours offered by members of the Asolo Theatre Guild. When you are in the balcony, walk up to the very top rows, just outside on the right hand side.

Listen very carefully. You too may hear the sighs emitted by the spirit of the old Dunfermline Opera House.

Consider too that there is yet another connection between Sarasota and Dunfermline.

The Scottish city, about an hour's drive north of Edinburgh, also was the home of Sir John Gillespie, one of Sarasota's founders and the father of Sarasota's first mayor, Col. J. Hamilton Gillespie, who also is known as the Father of American Golf. Both father and son are buried within two miles of the Asolo, at the old Rosemary Cemetery.

Incidentally, there is another way to experience a ghost.

Kim Cool

While waiting to meet McMullan, I asked the day guard of the Asolo, Jerry Richman, if he had ever experienced the Asolo's ghost.

"No, I never work nights." he said. "But the night watchman had an experience with the ghost just last week. The ghost scratched him."

Ghost of the Opera House

The Sarasota Opera House has its own spirits.

It also has a shared specter or two with the Golden Apple Dinner Theatre, according to several present-day opera house employees.

At least one dates to the building's earliest days as a host to silent pictures. "Skinners' Dress Suit," a silent picture starring Reginald Denny and Laura LaPlante, was shown at the grand opening of the old Edwards Theatre on April 10, 1926.

The film was accompanied by music from Dale Troy's Edwards Theatre Orchestra, songs by Edward's daughter, soprano Louise Phillips, and a performance by Samuel Ettelson on the theater's Robert Morton Orchestral Pipe Organ.

Despite the crash of the stock market and the end of the Florida land boom of the 1920s, the Edwards Theatre continued to be a mecca for first-class entertainment in Sarasota, playing host to the George White Scandals, the Ziegfeld Follies and such stars as Will Rogers, Tom Mix, W. C. Fields and the famous fan dancer, Sally Rand.

The ghosts of Ziegfeld, Rogers and other such celebrities of the day continue to make their presence known in the Sarasota area, especially at the winter home of their good friends, John and Mable Ringling.

These and many other spirits were discovered in that stately home by two mediums from the Church of the Angels in Venice. Those stories can be found in a later chapter of this book.

On Jan. 30, 1952, Cecil B. DeMille's film, "The Greatest Show on Earth," had its world premier at the theater.

The movie had been filmed in the Sarasota area and all its big stars were in town for the first showing.

One performer appeared four times at the theater on Feb. 21, 1956.

Although he has been seen nearly everywhere else since his death, I could find no sightings of Elvis Presley at the Sarasota Opera House.

Instead, there seems to be an unidentified spirit who is searching for a friend, according to a story related by an opera house employee who asked that I not use his name. The man has been associated with the building for years. While willing to pass on a tale or two, he said that he personally was not a believer in ghosts, that the mysterious sounds and strange happenings were just the sounds of an old building or of other people who might have been in the building at the same time. He said that even though there were times when he admitted that, to his knowledge, he had been the only person in the building.

His coworker was just the opposite. That man's beliefs are so strong that he refused to talk about the building at all except to say that the "opera house spirits are under control."

The first man went on to explain that the opera house and its next door neighbor, the Golden Apple Dinner Theatre, were said to share a ghost.

"The Golden Apple was part of us," he said, as he recounted the tale of a spirit that went back and forth from the Golden Apple building to the opera house

Kim Cool

complex.

Even today, the buildings share common walls and architectural styling as well as spirits

"It is probably someone looking for a friend," he had said of the elusive spirit the first time we spoke. "I had more experiences here in the Pavilion building than anywhere else. Some would make your hair stand up, especially late at night.

"Between 11:30 p.m. and midnight, you can often hear walking in the Peterson Great Room."

He admitted to hearing the sounds but, in my second interview with him, not to believing that the Great Room sounds were caused by opera house phantoms.

The room is in the Deanne Carroll Allyn Pavilion, the building between the Golden Apple Dinner Theatre and the Sarasota Opera House.

For whatever reason, by the time of my second interview with him, he had seemingly changed his outlook on things that go bump in the night.

Hopefully it will put his mind at ease to learn that, in the 1990s a chimera figure, an architectural adornment thought to ward off evil, replaced the original "imp" on the North corner of the building.

The Sarasota Opera House and its Deane Carroll Allyn Pavilion fill nearly an entire block across from Five Points Park. and west of the Sarasota Golden Apple Dinner Theatre.

Part II
Singular Spirits

Photo by Kim Cool
The Burns Family plot at Rosemary Cemetery which is located within sight of the city's Utility Department, site of at least one "singular spirit," according to employee Rafael Perez.

49

Kim Cool

Probable cause

Sarasota city employee Debbie Perez is typical of many people.

She is open-minded enough to admit to the possibility, even the probability of the existence of ghosts, but she generally looks for logical explanations when strange things occur.

For 15 years she has worked in the old municipal auditorium on North Tamiami Trail. The old quonset-hut style building is the source of many strange sounds, creaking noises, even the sound of the wind rustling through the cavernous space. Perez has always discounted those sounds as just the normal sounds emitted by such an old building.

One incident that occurred at her mother-in-law's house was another thing altogether, one that she could not write off to any explainable reason.

The unexplainable incident occurred some months after the death of her father-in-law.

Her mother-in-law said she heard someone enter the house. She even heard the distinct swishing of his pant legs rubbing together as he walked toward the kitchen. Going to the kitchen to see who was there, the mother-in-law saw no one.

Then, shortly after that unexplainable incident, Debbie had a personal experience that she said still gives her pause.

"Just talking about it gives me goose bumps," she said.

Debbie was at home in her own house but she smelled the distinctive aroma of her aunt's home. The lady had died some months earlier, her favorite aunt, the one who died too young and too soon.

"I also felt a chill in the air, in the top part of the room," she said. "I called to my aunt and then I called my husband to come into the room and he sensed the chilly air too."

Smells and chilly air are common characteristics of paranormal occurrences.

Debbie's husband, Rafael, came into the hallway where Debbie was at the time. He said he did not notice the distinctive aroma that she had experienced but that he did feel the chill in the air.

"Heat rises, yet it was cold at the top of the room, not the bottom," she said.

There was no other explanation except that it must have been her aunt.

Unlike his wife, Rafael has had several unexplained occurrences at his job site.

"They hear footsteps and a door closing and other sounds," she said. "They swear there is something there. There also is an old cemetery behind the water treatment plant."

Rafael works for the Sarasota Water Department. The building, on 12th Street, happens to overlook the old Rosemary Cemetery but experts in the field of ghost hunting, writers like Charles J. Adams III and Rosemary Ellen Guiley, say that ghosts are rarely seen in cemeteries. Instead they are more likely to be seen where they died (on a battlefield, for example) or possibly someplace where they left an imprint while alive. What can be seen at the old Rosemary Cemetery are the graves of the city's first mayor, John Hamilton Gillespie, early real estate developer Owen Burns and several members of their families.

Judging by the experiences of Rafael and his co-worker, a man named Bob, several people must have left imprints at the water department.

"I was in the kitchen," Rafael said. "I heard steps. And then when I was in the control room I heard more steps in the hallway and the sound of keys rattling.

"Then I heard the sound of laughter in one of the rooms but when I looked out, there was no one there."

On another occasion, Rafael said he was taking readings in the control room when he felt that someone was there, beside him.

"It was an eerie feeling," he said. "It makes you want to get the readings and get out of there — fast."

Rafael was concerned enough that he called his friend Maggie Sumney who is a paranormal researcher — a ghost hunter. She came with some of her fellow researchers but they didn't find anything.

On another occasion, a friend had a pet dachshund with him, in a cage. The dog seemed to be looking through the window into the control room and he was barking like mad at something he saw in the window. There was nothing there.

While strange and seemingly unexplainable, these incidents may or may not indicate paranormal activity.

The last incident related by Rafael has no other explanation.

This tale involved a t-bar, a heavy steel rod, that is used by the water department workers to open valves.

"It was leaning against one of the support beams in the building," Rafael said. "It was 11 a.m. in the morning and for no reason, the t-bar had fallen.

"That would not be unusual except that it fell the opposite direction from which it was leaning."

This rod was indoors. There was no wind. There was nothing that would have caused it to fall in either direction, let alone away from the wall against which it had been propped — nothing except perhaps a powerful poltergeist!

Visiting ghost

Sarasota, like many cities in Florida, especially those along the coasts or near the big theme parks, has more visitors than full-time residents.

Some visitors, called snowbirds, divide their time between their Florida homes and their northern homes. Others come occasionally, usually for just one or two weeks.

Nearly all find reasons to return again and again, for the sun, the sand, the arts, the beautiful sunsets, or simply to visit family.

For some, the lure is so great, they continue to visit

Kim Cool

their favorite Florida haunts even after they have passed on to some other realm.

The news editor of the *Venice Gondolier Sun*, Pat Garlusky Horwell, lives in Sarasota. Her father was one of those occasional visitors. Since his death, it seems he has continued to return to the land of sunshine.

Like Pat, her father was an avid player of card games, especially Solitaire.

Pat, like many writers, spends a lot of time on her home computer. Too often, while waiting for the printer to complete its work, she has idle time on her hands.

On those occasions, she plays computer solitaire.

As the game's name implies, she plays alone — but not always. Sometimes her father comes to help her for that is another thing about that game, it is hard to watch someone else play the game alone. Most people try to jump in and offer advice. Parents seem to be especially adept at jumping in to offer advice or a helping hand.

"Every so often I know he is there," she said. "The other night I was playing Solitaire and I kept winning.

"When the evening was over I had racked up more than 1,000 points. He was there helping me."

Pat was referring to her father.

This was not the first time that she had sensed her father was with her, in Sarasota, or elsewhere. Shortly

56

after his funeral, Pat and a friend were driving back to Sarasota from Jacksonville.

They had been at a conference for a few days.

They were tired even before climbing into the car for the five-hour drive back to Sarasota.

Pat was driving and she grew more tired as the hours ticked by.

Suddenly, she felt an arm on her back.

"It was like someone was rubbing the back of my neck," she said. "I looked over at Jim and he was leaning against the side of the car, sound asleep. His hands were in his lap.

"I knew it was my father."

He was looking out for her, making sure she did not fall asleep at the wheel, she said.

The night she was playing so much Solitaire, he was there again, helping her to win because she needed to win that night.

Everyone needs to have his or her spirits bolstered occasionally.

For Pat, that was the night.

Pat said her father had been particularly skilled at Solitaire and was quite capable of helping her win more games. She said she was convinced that he was the one behind her winning ways that night.

Kim Cool

Finally, when her work was done, she thanked her father for helping her with her games and decided to keep on playing since she was having such a run of luck.

She had not reckoned on her father sending her a second message.

"I started losing every game and my score was nearly back to zero," she said. "It was his way of letting me know that he was still the best player."

Pelican man's dovecote

This ghost story is a little different. It is about a man who died twice but might more accurately be described as a future ghost.

Dale Shields became known as "the Pelican Man" in the 1980s after he rescued his first pelican.

At his death, on Jan. 2, 2003, the Pelican Man's Bird Sanctuary in Sarasota had rescued more than 150,000 birds and animals.

At precisely the moment that one of those rescued birds was released, the call came that Shields had passed on.

Kim Cool

The man who, like Dr. Doolittle, could talk to the animals, had died for the second time.

The first time he died was shortly after he had rescued that first pelican. While fishing for fresh food for the injured bird, Shields had a heart attack, ended up in the hospital and, when stricken with a second heart attack, he died.

For a brief time he was "clinically dead."

That time he was revived.

Afterwards he told everyone that he remembered everything that happened to him while he was dead. He said that he went to Heaven, saw many birds there and actually heard God. He said that he promised God that if he lived he would devote his life to saving pelicans and other wildlife.

With his new lease on life, Shields kept his promise, building a wildlife sanctuary that is unique in the United States, if not the world.

That first pelican, by the name of George, also survived and was eventually released back into the wild. One month later, George the pelican returned with his entire bird family — nearly 200 pelicans. True to his word, the Pelican Man began his work, moving onto City Island to build his sanctuary in 1988, eventually enlisting the help of more than 300 volunteers and sev-

The Pelican Man, Dale Shields, aboard the Peli-Boat on a Halloween shortly before Halloween 2002.

eral million dollars in donations from all over the world.

That his death coincided with the release of one of his rescued birds can only be taken as a sign that his work will go on.

Since his death, one pelican has been seen hovering in the air over the sanctuary on several occasions.

Is it Shields? Is he making sure that his creatures are being cared for and that his work is continuing?

I think so.

Longtime sanctuary volunteer Alison Guess thinks so too.

"When they built the flight cage, they built a dove house on top," she said a few weeks after Sheilds' death. "They did it so that when Dale died he would always have a home for his spirit to come to."

The flight cage is a rather large screen-walled wooden structure in which the larger birds are encouraged to fly to see if their wings are strong enough, before the birds are released to the wild. It is right behind the Bird of Prey area at the sanctuary, Guess said.

I asked her if Sheilds knew about the Dove house.

"Yes, Dale knew about it," she said. "His spirit will always be in the sanctuary."

Part III

Neighborhoods

Kim Cool

Indian Beach spirits

The Evans backyard may harbor three dancing Calusa Indians but the rest of their tribe along with some Creeks and other Native Americans seem to be in the Indian Beach neighborhood of Sarasota.

Bounded by the John and Mable Ringling Museum of Art complex on the north and Indian Beach Drive on the South, the neighborhood is nestled between U.S. 41 (the Tamiami Trail) on the east and Sarasota Bay on the west. Dotted with magnificent homes to this day, the area was "the place to live" during the 1920s land boom, drawing wealthy buyers from New York and

Ghost Stories of Sarasota

Photo by Kim Cool

Artist Rilla Fleming has painted a series of paintings featuring the banyan tree behind Ca d'Zan, the winter home of John and Mable Ringling in the Indian Beach neighborhood of Sarasota. She lives in the Towles Court area. Both areas are reported to be haunted.

65

Kim Cool

such Sarasota movers and shakers as John and Charles Ringling and their friend Ralph Caples.

Their homes remain, well preserved testaments to a gilded age. Like all of Sarasota, this neighborhood has a variety of home styles and sizes, built from the 1920s right up until this year.

Illinois native Anne Cederberg lives in that neighborhood. By day she works as an educator and guide at the Pelican Man Bird Sanctuary in Sarasota.

By night, she digs into the history of the area, especially its haunted history.

"There are Indian mounds there," she said. "Nearby is Whitaker Bayou, one of the few hills in Sarasota."

Sarasota's first white settlers lived in that area, including Bill Whitaker who arrived in 1842 as a home-steader, receiving 160 acres of land under the Armed Occupation Act of 1842. Whitaker's land had fresh spring water, a high bluff called Yellow Bluffs and a bayou or inlet running through the property. The young settler weathered at least two fearsome hurricanes on his land, including the 1848 storm which was dubbed the "granddaddy of all hurricanes."

That storm was the one that created a new opening through Longboat Key. Whitaker called the opening New Pass, its name to this day.

At home in Holmes Beach

One of the best things about amassing stories for a book such as this is the people you meet.

One of these special people is Kim Noah, an employee of Circle Books, a charming little book store on St. Armands Circle in Sarasota.

After hours, she pursues her study of anthropology, sometimes in Sarasota and sometimes in Croatia where she is helping to resurrect the history of that war-ravaged country. In Sarasota, she and a good friend have worked with public and private citizens to document the city's past from an archeological viewpoint as well as from an historical viewpoint.

Kim Cool

Along the way she also has developed an interest in ghost stories.

It is a family thing.

Kim said she has a cousin who is interested in paranormal phenomena and that she had an Italian grandmother who was an exorcist in Italy.

"Nine times out of 10, what seems like it might be ghosts is just one's imagination," she said. "But sometimes the stories are valid."

As an illustration she related the story of a mother and daughter and a house in Holmes Beach on Anna Maria Island. She described the house as a typical one-story, two-bedroom house, not unlike most of the houses in Florida, of whatever vintage.

She learned this story from the daughter who approached her one day after hearing that she was interested in ghost stories. Kim was working at a department store in Sarasota and attending American University in Washington, D.C. during the school year.

"I was 19 at the time and the daughter was 26," Kim said. "She asked me if I would be interested in visiting the house."

It was the third house to be rented by the mother and daughter in a very short period of time.

"It was as though something was following them,"

Kim said. "The mother studies demonology and is wheelchair bound.

"Shortly after they moved in, the daughter was awakened in the middle of the night. She saw her grandmother sitting on the edge of the other bed across the room."

The grandmother was deceased and Kim asked the young lady if she could have been dreaming.

The young girl said that she was not dreaming and was convinced that she really had seen her grandmother,

When it happened a second time, the young lady asked Kim if she would spend the night in the house.

"I brought my Bible," Kim said. "I was raised a Catholic and whenever I go to a house that might be haunted, I carry my Bible.

"Nothing happened during the night. But the next morning there were several strange phenomena. I had also brought an exercise tape and we were in the living room, seated on the floor doing stretching exercises."

As they watched the tape and began their warm-ups, crashing sounds came from the kitchen.

"They had a lot of copper pots and pans," Kim said. "They didn't use them for cooking but for decorating their kitchen.

"While we were in the living room, they all flew off the wall and across the room.

"No one was in the kitchen at the time.

"Then a few minutes later, while still seated on the floor, we noticed that the shag carpeting was becoming very wet."

Again there was no rational explanation, Kim said. There was no leak anywhere and the carpeting was too wet to have been caused by the damp air from the near-by beach.

And there was one other thing that spooked Kim.

"It was something the mother told me the night before," Kim said. "She saw a dog in the house, moving backwards. It moved backwards into the hall and then it disappeared."

Deciding that a vanishing dog, flying copper pots and wet carpeting were too much for her to handle, she decided to call her priest and get him involved.

Kim also related a story about another house near the beach. This house is on Whitfield not far from the Bay Shore area where she grew up.

"It is a very notorious house," she said. "The guy who owns it can't sell it and he can't rent it. No one wants to live there because it is so haunted."

If no one rents it there will be more room for ghosts.

Little in common

While house-hunting in Sarasota, Kelly Fores befriended a ghost.

Actually it was to be some time before he would become either a friend or a ghost.

"I just knocked on the door and asked if he knew how old the roof was on the house next door," she said. "And can you tell me about the people who used to live there?"

Fores was house hunting in the neighborhood and figured the next door neighbor might share some information about the house.

71

It turned out the man was a roofer so his information on the home's roof was probably pretty good.

Fores bought the house and moved in. The house, built in 1973, is in the DeSoto Lakes area of Sarasota, near the dog track and east of the airport, off Lockwood Ridge Road. The neighbor's house was built about 1980.

"He was a biker and basically we had nothing in common," she said.

Fores enrolled her daughter in school and started work as the media relations director for the Asolo Theatre Company. She had little or no contact with the biker although she did learn his name, Dick Tracy, just like the famous cartoon character. But this Dick Tracy wore biker clothes. He did not wear a black Fedora and a yellow overcoat like the character in the movie.

Though neighbors, each went their separate ways.

Then, in the fall of 2001, Tropical Storm Gabrielle blew through Sarasota County, inflicting $15 million in damage and dropping a large pine tree on Fores' house.

A second pine tree had smashed into her neighbor's roof.

"While we were outside cleaning up the debris, we became reacquainted," she said. "My dad gave me new siding for the house and my neighbor asked where I got the siding because he wanted the same siding for his house."

Ghost Stories of Sarasota

Besides chatting about the siding, they also chatted about his friend's big and "barky" dog.

Over the next few weeks they found themselves outside at the same time fairly often. Fores and her dad would be working on her house and Tracy and his friend were putting a new metal roof on his house to replace the one damaged by Gabrielle.

"He had put roofs on buildings all over Sarasota," Fores said. "One day, he was just sitting up on the roof with his friend and my dad yelled to him, 'You're not working.'"

A few days later Tracy put a card in Fores' door. It was marked, "good for one dinner."

They went out for one dinner and then another. One day he invited her to share a steak that was too big for one and soon they were in a routine of eating together fairly often. Sometimes he would bring his two boys over or she would bring her daughter over and they would all eat together.

While dining together, she discovered that she and the biker/roofer actually had a lot in common despite the 20-year difference in their ages. She also learned that he was very well traveled.

"He had just returned from a month in Russia," Fores said, "It was only about three weeks later and I

73

was coming home from work when I saw all these people in the road near my house.

"My friend Becky motioned me to pull over and she told me that Dick had fallen off the roof.

"Just that morning he had invited me in for coffee and I had said to him, 'I'll see you later.'"

They had taken him to a local church parking lot and were going to Bay-flight him to the hospital in Tampa Bay.

Fores was left in charge of locking up the house after the police had finished their business at the site.

"I actually think I knew he was dead before his sister did," Fores said. "Nobody who had seen it happen really knew. He had fallen off the lowest part of the roof which was only 8 feet off the ground. I didn't think it would be that bad.

"I had told the policeman I was just his neighbor but when he (the policeman) said it was bad news and that he didn't make it, I hit the ground. Then I was clinging to the detective and sobbing.

"He (Tracy) was just 50."

When Fores called her father to tell him that Tracy was dead, her father knew, even before she told him.

Later that night, Tracy's sister asked Fores to watch the house and his pet sugar gliders until they could make other arrangements.

Fores was glad to do that and went right over that night.

"I wanted to be there," she said. "away from the nosy neighbors. While was there, I found his Harley bandanna and said that he needed to be buried with that."

And then she yelled at him, angry that he, a professional roofer, would have been so careless to have fallen.

As she kept on cleaning up the debris left by the paramedics outside, she kept talking to Tracy and finally asked him to "give me a sign that you know I am talking to you."

There was no one in the house and his bedroom blinds had been shut forever but all of a sudden, the blinds were open, she said.

"It stopped me in my tracks because I had never seen them open," she said, "and the next day they were shut again. No one was in the house.

On another day, she was sitting on the lanai and happened to pick up a deck of cards that was there. The bottom card was some nondescript card like a three or four of clubs. The next day, she was again seated on the lanai, and again picked up the same deck of cards. This time, the bottom card was a Queen of hearts.

No one else had been in the house and all she could think was "Who is messing with me?"

Then she started thinking that if only she had come home earlier, it might not have happened.

As if he had read her thoughts, Tracy sent her a message.

She thought it was a dream or maybe an out of body experience.

"He was laughing and saying, 'I'm happy where I am. Don't mourn for me.'"

That made her think of another time when she had held a conversation with a spirit — her grandmother. At the time she thought it might have been a dream but later she realized that she had helped her grandmother cross over into Heaven,

"It was late at night and I saw my grandmother in a tunnel filled with white light," Fores said. "I told her to go toward the light, that she would be all right.

"The next morning my mother called me and told me that my grandmother had died the preceding night."

That is when she realized it was more than just a dream.

Fores has seen other ghosts too, She said she was almost killed by one nasty ghost when she was going to high school in Wisconsin. Consequently, talking to her neighborly ghost did not seem strange to her.

"After I moved out of my parents' house, my dad said that I had brought a lot of activity to the house," Fores said.

Her father was referring to ghostly activity.

She seems to have brought similar activity to Sarasota where she found a friend and a ghost, all in one.

The relationship started because of one roof (hers) and ended because of another roof (his).

"The fact that he was a professional made it all the worse," she said.

The fact that she has psychic powers made it all the better.

Kim Cool

Where there's smoke

In the same general neighborhood where Dick Tracy lived, there is another house that seems to contain a spirit.

This spook pays no attention to the dangers of cigarette smoking, cheerfully puffing away late at night after the livelier occupants of the house have gone to bed.

The story was told to be by Rilla Fleming, a Sarasota artist who also happens to have strong psychic abilities. She also shared a great deal of information about some of the spirits to be found at Ca d'Zan, the former home of John and Mable Ringling but that is another story.

The puffing poltergeist dwells in an old stucco house on Old Bradenton Road, in the vicinity of the Sarasota Kennel Club. Rilla's step brother and his family lived in the house until very recently.

"Kevin and Annie had a rocking chair in the living room," Rilla said. "They often would see it rocking on its own even though there was no wind or anything else that might have caused the chair to begin rocking."

They were not afraid of the rocking chair and soon got used to it. What they had more trouble adjusting to happened late at night, after they had gone to bed.

"They would smell cigarette smoke." Rilla said. "They would even see the smoke when they got up to check on things and they would find cigarette butts in the ashtrays in the morning."

Somehow they knew it was a female ghost, Rilla continued.

"Her spirit was there."

Rilla also told of two houses on the other side of town, on Sarasota Boulevard, just north of Sarasota Jungle Gardens.Looking like mini castles, the nearly twin houses had been built for some midgets in the circus.

No longer inhabited by circus people, these two houses still have a mystical quality she said.

Kim Cool

For arts' sake

There are many artistic enclaves in Sarasota.

Palm Avenue is lined with galleries.

In the vicinity of Main Street, Palm and Pineapple avenues, boutiques, several theaters, bookshops and the Opera House co-mingle.

North of there, along the North Tamiami Trail, one can find the Van Wezel Performing Arts Hall, the Sarasota Garden Center, the Ringling School of Design and the Florida State University campus which houses the John and Mable Ringling Museum of Art, ca d'Zan, the Museum of the Circus and the FSU Center for the

Performing Arts, the home of the Asolo Theatre
Company, the FSU/Asolo Conservatory of Actor
Training and the Sarasota Ballet of Florida.

To the east, but still in the heart of old Sarasota, within the city's Laurel Park neighborhood, is Towles Court
Artist Colony.

Named for the Chicago businessman who built the
bungalow style cottages in the early 1920s, the area lan-
guished for years after the Great Depression wreaked its
havoc on the area. Finally a group of artists, led by
Kathleen Carrillo, resurrected the area to accommodate
the needs of artists.

Artists and performers live in every area of the city
but no other area of the city can match this place for its
spirituality and its mystic qualities.

"This area is more than spiritual," artist Rilla
Fleming said, "It is sacred."

She took me to the center of Towles Court and point-
ed to the oak trees and a bunch of signs just outside the
Katherine Butler Gallery, just about at the center of
Towles Court.

"There is something about those trees and this
place," she said before walking with me to Carrillo's studio and home.

Carrillo agreed and took me through her house to

her back yard along Morrill Street. There, she pointed to two cypress trees, one on either side of her house, standing like matching sentinels pointing the way to the center of Towles Court.

"Cypress trees do not live more than 100 years," she said. "Those trees have been checked by arborists. They are 300 years old."

If one drew a line from one cypress tree to the other and then to the sacred spot pointed out by Fleming and from there to the first cypress tree, I think it would make nearly an equilateral triangle. I am not sure what that means but while I was standing in Carrillo's house, it seemed very important, as though it really is a sacred site.

Actually, it was a sacred site to the Native Americans who lived in the area hundreds of years earlier, Carrillo said.

"They performed religious ceremonies there," she said. It was their most sacred place."

Carrillo built her house next to that sacred site, adding it on behind the little bungalow that she uses as her gallery. But before she built the house and before she opened the gallery, she had her friend, a guru named Frank LoVerde, check out the site.

"He told me to make it happen," she said. "He said

Artist Cathleen Carillo holds her hand above the geometric center of her home and studio Towles Court Artist Colony. The unusual two-way crack appeared directly above a magic crystal implanted in the home's concrete base during construction.

that in this time and space, all the people that were here in a past life are coming together now in this life.

"When I decided to build, I was studying Feng Shui (the Oriental art of placement) and Katherine Carsly called me up and asked if she could come by with her class and bless the site."

Carrillo said she didn't know her at the time but was

happy to have the blessing.

She followed that by depositing blessings, essential oils and crystals in the foundation before the cement slab was built. On the day the cement was poured, she asked one of the concrete workers to "do something for me."

Carrillo had a box filled with more blessings, essential oils and another crystal. She wanted that to be buried within the slab at the center of her property.

"He was a big burly guy and I told him I would have to anoint him with essential oils too," she said. "He was adorable. He told the other guys not to say a word about it to anyone and then he placed the box in the center of the foundation."

Carrillo then walked me over to the spot which had been so well blessed. She has tile floors throughout her house. At the exact spot where she pointed, the tile was cracked in two directions, exactly 90 degrees off.

"For two years I worked really hard to attract people here," she said. "Now it's shaking out. The people who don't belong are falling out and the people who do are coming in.

"Since I have been here, my work has completely changed. My pieces are magic. My work transcends my experience. Spirit works through me."

Carrillo said her work sells for three times as much as it did and she attributes that to the space.

She led me into the gallery and showed me an example, "Renaissance of Light."

Several people seem to be trying to fly. The background is Venice, italy, which she visited a few months earlier.

"The woman in the piece has let go and is flying," Carrillo said. "She is moving into the light."

LoVerde also has moved into the light. He passed away in 2002.

I had first been to the gallery about four years earlier. Carrillo's paintings had changed, taking on a more magical quality.

As I left her gallery, I recognized something about myself in relation to Towles Court. In my job as the features editor of the *Venice Gondolier Sun*, I go everywhere in search of stories for day trips. That is what brought me to Towles Court for the first time four years earlier. Rarely do I return to any of those places for personal reasons. Yet I had returned to Towles Court many times, always bringing friends along so they too could see my "find."

Like the Beatles, I had experienced a "Magical Mystery Tour."

Kim Cool

The ghost of Lido Key

In ghost hunting, it makes sense to take the obvious routes. Visit old buildings and places where important things have happened, places where people have left imprints as they have passed by.

Sarasota has several historic buildings, Indian burial areas and places like the former winter home of the Ringling Bros. Barnum & Bailey Circus. All these places seemed to be likely sites for specter spotting.

Old hotels often house ghosts.

So do newer hotels as it turns out.

Just before Christmas 2002, Sarasota visitors Joe

Bookalam and his wife were staying at the Radisson Hotel on Lido Key when they learned about that hotel's resident spirit from two hotel employees.

"There had been a fatality in Room 104," Bookalam said. "The room was in the north tower of the hotel, the older tower.

"Afterwards there were several reports of strange things happening in that room. Eventually, the cleaning ladies refused to clean that room.

"So, they got rid of the room."

Whether or not they got rid of the spirit is something else altogether according to a psychic named Lady Jerry who was staying at the hotel during the same week that the Bookalams were in residence.

And who would blame any ghost, spirit, specter or wraith for wanting to remain at the Radisson, given its perfect location for vacationers to Sarasota.

I have no doubt there are other ghost guests at hotels up and down the beaches of Sarasota although I could not find a single hotel or motel manager who would admit to having experienced any such entities.

Most helpful was a lady named Vicky Hadley, owner of The Cypress, a bed and breakfast on Gulf Stream Avenue. She said there was a story about the former owner of the property, a woman who had refused to sell her house even for a million dollars. Known as "The hold-out, " the lady was a heroine, maintaining the one and only house in an area that is otherwise filled with high-rise condos and hotels.

"There is a nice feeling in the house," Vicky said. "It is the only house left. She wouldn't even take a million dollars for it."

Perhaps that warm feeling is attributable to the spirit of "The hold-out." Her spirit will continue to be happy as long as the property's owners follow in her footsteps, holding out against any and all offers.

Vicky put me in touch with another B&B owner, Liz Stanford. Stanford is renovating her three-suite B&B on Vamo Drive near Sarasota Square Mall.

Stanford said she had not had any ghostly experiences but was sure there must be a ghost in the Villa at Raintree because it was old enough, having been built in 1924. Since this book went to press before the renovations were complete, all I can do is suggest that you might stop by and do some ghost hunting there yourself.

With or without ghosts, it still stands.

That is not the case with Sarasota's oldest ghost hotel.

The ghost hotel was John Ringling's most ambitious project.

He had built his somewhat Moorish Mediterranean

Revival or Venetian Gothic mansion, Ca d'Zan, along the shore of the Gulf of Mexico. He also had built the John and Mable Ringling Museum of Art, purchased St. Armands Circle and built a $1 million causeway connecting St. Armand's to the mainland. Sarasota, thanks to Ringling, was on the map, becoming more well known, day by day.

A Ritz Carlton Hotel would be the final proof that Sarasota was all that Ringling had envisioned.

In March, 1927, as the Florida land boom was beginning to lose some of its steam and the Great Depression was looming just off the horizon, Ringling broke ground on Longboat Key for what he hoped would cap his real estate career.

Instead, the dominoes began to fall, one by one. The Florida land boom ended that fall, just months after construction had begun.

Construction stalled and when the stock market crashed just one year later, the death knell sounded for the 250-room hotel.

It never housed a paying guest, nor a ghost, although it may have hosted a few transients over the years.

Instead, the hotel itself was a ghostly apparition of what might have been and it would remain in that state for nearly 40 years.

Kim Cool

Finally, in 1964 another generation of developers demolished the building to make way for a new resort. Only Ringling's dream remained.

But it would be another 37 years before Sarasota would finally get its Ritz Carlton and the city would lose two other ghost buildings in the process; the John Ringling Towers and the historic Bickel House. Both were demolished to make way for the new hotel.

Also gone is a small cemetery that once held the graves of Ringling employees, including two who were reported to have died from accidental causes during the construction of Ca d'Zan.

While the ghost buildings and the graves have vanished, memories remain and possibly a few ghosts.

The original name of the John Ringling Towers was the Hotel Vernona. It had been built by Owen Burns and named for his wife Vernona. The name was kept for the restaurant in the new Ritz Carlton Sarasota. and the name of Ringling's home was borrowed for the hotel's cigar bar.

Ringling never lived to see this dream of a Ritz-Carlton Hotel for Sarasota come true.

But that is not to say that he has not seen the new hotel.

There have been many reports of John Ringling

sightings and not all of them at his former home.

People have been heard playing cards very late at night in the new hotel's cigar bar. They have been heard but they have not been seen. Perhaps he occasionally leaves the house of his dreams to visit the hotel of his dreams.

The Bickel House had been built in 1925, designed by Dwight James Baum for a realty company. Karl Bickel, owner of United Press, had the building converted into his home in 1933. He lived in the house until 1949. Despite its prime location at 101 North Tamiami Trail and its 1987 listing on the National Register of Historic Places, the house stood vacant in its later years, until it too was demolished about two years after the John Ringling Towers when no one could be found who was willing to move it elsewhere.

Baum also designed the El Vernona-Broadway Apartments at 1133 4th St. That building also was destined for ghostdom.

And, it could well be that all the ghosts of those old buildings found their way to Ca d'Zan on the night of Feb. 4, 2003. As you will read in Chapter 8, hundreds of spirits were there that night, many with plans of crossing over.

Part IV
Indian Spirits

Dance, dance, dance

Lisa and Mike Evans live in a circa 1951 house on Loma Linda Road in Sarasota. Their neighbors include three Calusa Indians, long dead, possibly for as long as 5,000 years.

The Calusas are thought to be the first human inhabitants of Florida, living up and down along the state's West Coast from about 3000 B.C. until the 16th century.

Theirs was a highly evolved society that lived off the fruits of the sea rather than the land, and traded with the Tekesta Indians on the Atlantic Coast of Florida.

By the time Spanish explorer Juan Ponce De Leon

arrived in 1513, there were nearly 100,000 Native Americans, including more than 20,000 Calusas.

They traveled as far as the Caribbean in huge dugout boats, lived in open-sided Chickees built on stilts as protection against high tides and celebrated their religious festivals with elaborate ceremonies which involved dancing and the wearing of fanciful masks depicting animal and human spirits.

All these years later, three of the tribe are still dancing — in the backyard of the Evans' home.

That just three Calusa ghosts remain could well be related to Ponce de Leon's arrival.

In less than 20 years after the arrival of the explorers and the settlers who followed, the Native American population had dwindled to less than 11,000, mostly Creeks.

After Indian wars, exposure to diseases unknown to the Native Americans and deportation to out-of-state reservations there were less than 70 Calusas in Florida, almost exclusively in the Everglades.

It may never be known if the Evans' Calusa dancers are some of the last Calusas or some of the earliest ones.

What did remain for many years were the Calusa middens (mounds). Most of the middens up and down the West Coast of Florida were trash heaps and contained little more than shards of pottery interspersed with piles of seashells. The shells may have been the residue of their meals.

There also were a few burial mounds.

But like the Calusas themselves, even the middens were destined to disappear.

As colonists and developers ravaged the land to plant crops and build homes and even towns and cities, the middens were bull-dozed.

Today, there are very few intact middens. Some at Indian Mound Park in Englewood and some at Historic Spanish Point in Osprey, south of the city of Sarasota plus a very few at other spots on barrier islands along the Gulf coast. At Historic Spanish Point, visitors can peer into a cutaway view of a real midden, seeing the various strata of refuse that remains. In addition to the scant number of middens, there are a few fragments of masks, figurines and their artwork and ceremonial items in a few museums.

"I have been to a native American museum," Lisa said. "I recognized these Indians. They are the same ones I saw in the museum."

The homes on Loma Linda were mostly built in the 1950s and if there was an Indian midden (whether burial mound or trash heap) it was removed then or even earlier.

Kim Cool

Lisa is pretty sure the Evans' house was built on a midden because whenever she digs in the backyard she finds shells and things that might have been in a midden....but no bones.

"If anyone found bones while building or remodeling, work would stop immediately," she said.

But nothing stops the Indian spirits.

"I have seen them," she said. "so have most of my neighbors."

They dance around in the Evans' back yard, as if they are protecting something or someone.

According to the legends of the Calusas, their people possess three souls. One soul is the pupil of the eye. The second soul is one's shadow and the last is one's mirror image. The Calusas believed that one of these souls would stay with the body after death.

The Evans do not feel threatened.

Instead, they feel protected.

These three Calusas seem to be doing their job.

Part V
Circus Ghosts

THE FIVE RINGLING BROTHERS

ALBERT, OTTO, ALFRED, CHARLES, AND JOHN. BEGINNING WI
SMALL WAGON SHOW THEY ROSE OVER THE YEARS TO TH
THE CIRCUS WORLD. THEIR CROWNING ACHIEVEMENT CA
HEN THEY BOUGHT THEIR CHIEF RIVAL – BARNUM & BAI
ON COMBINING IT WITH THEIR OWN THRIVING CIRCUS, T
EATED AN ENDURING INSTITUTION KNOWN AS RINGLING
D BARNUM & BAILEY, "THE GREATEST SHOW ON EARTH"

FRIENDS OF THE RINGLINGS

Dusty's best friend

When Cecil B. DeMille was looking for the perfect place to film the outdoor scenes of his spectacular film, "The Greatest Show on Earth," it was only natural that he chose Sarasota.

The grand opening scene of the film was filmed in Sarasota," former Ringling acrobat Alvin Schwartz said. "The parade was filmed in Venice and the train wreck in Sarasota."

For more than 30 years Sarasota had been the home of the Greatest Show on Earth. The Ringling Bros. and Barnum & Bailey Circus. Even today, the town is home to some 16 circuses that winter in the area.

But, all together, those 16 circuses do not compare with the greatest circus of them all, the Ringling Bros. and Barnum & Bailey Circus which had been brought to Sarasota originally by John and Charles Ringling in the late 1920s.

"Thank you John Ringling," animal trainer and Ringling performance director John Herriott said before the 2003 installation ceremonies for the city's Circus Ring of Fame on St. Armand's Circle. "If not for him, we would all be living in some very cold place like Pennsylvania or Indiana."

Or even Baraboo, Wisconsin, which housed the Ringling show briefly after it left Venice and before it returned to Florida.

Herriott is now semi-retired.

Herriott said that he thought there were more circus people living in the Sarasota-Venice area now than at any time since the Ringling show first came to Sarasota.

While he said he has not seen any ghosts, he did speak about the day he revisited the old circus arena in Venice.

"The gate was open and I could see the ring barn," he said. "It was like something out of the twilight zone."

After the induction ceremonies, I met dog trainer Dusty Sadler, a performer with the Clyde Beatty-Cole Bros. Circus.

Kim Cool

Photo by Kim Cool
Circus animal trainer Dusty Sadler shared his ghost story after the 2002 induction ceremonies of the Circus Ring of Fame in St. Armands Circle, Sarasota.

Though smaller than the Ringling show, it is considered the largest circus in America that is still performed in a tent. Sadler has had a dog act with the circus for more than one quarter of a century.

Like Herriott, he is happy to be living in Sarasota.

He has a house near the Sarasota Bradenton Airport, in an area where I unearthed a few stories that wound their way into this book. There is no other connection than the location.

Dusty lives in his house with his dog Bailey T and

Ghost Stories of Sarasota

special memories of Toby, his first canine partner in the dog act.

Toby was a Cocker Spaniel with black splotches. Bailey T is nearly identical.

"Toby and I had an act together for eight years," Dusty said. "Then Toby developed a heart condition and had to retire. She lived another eight years."

Dusty had her cremated and keeps the cremains in his house, in a special box.

Eventually he got another dog and decided to continue the act. That new dog was Bailey T.

"Bailey T. looks just like Toby," Dusty said.

One day Dusty was folding napkins in the kitchen.

"There was a Teddy bear design on the napkins," he said. "except for one napkin. Instead of the bear, it was Toby, with angel wings."

Right before his eyes, the design had changed. That one napkin had Toby's face where all the others had Teddy bears.

Dusty folded that napkin very carefully. Cradling it very carefully, he put it in the box with Toby's cremains.

As it turned out, that was simply the first Toby sighting.

"One night I was at home watching television and I heard a gurgling sound," he continued. "I have one of

101

those water dishes with a bottle that refills the dish.

"When I heard the gurgling sound, I looked over. There was this clear-liquid-like form of a dog. I could see its head and most of its body and it was drinking from the water dish.

Carole Lee, a Venice medium said that Dusty's description is consistent with a certain type of spirit.

"Toby was a big water drinker. I sat there stunned, but pleased," Dusty said.

Dusty has continued to see Toby from time to time.

A few weeks later, he was sure that he had seen Bailey T dash through the kitchen but when he went into the living room, he found Bailey T asleep in a chair.

"It's like Toby is constantly with me," Dusty said. "I was so close to that dog."

Dusty said he is convinced that Toby sent Bailey to him.

"The T in Bailey T's name is for Toby," he said.

Obviously Toby was a great believer in that old show business adage, "The show must go on."

So was Jackie St. Clair, the only living clown to have been honored at The Ring of Fame in Sarasota.

Jackie has fond memories of the cameraderie on the performers in the circus.

He grew up in the circus and especially remembers a

night when he was 16 and there was a terrible storm that really shook the tent and scared the daylights out of him.

"What'll I do, Daddy?" he cried to his father who also was a performer in the Ringling show.

"From then on, every time there was a really bad storm, everyone in the circus would cry, "What'll I do, Daddy?"

St. Clair said the performers were a very superstitious lot. They would not wear yellow, calling it a Jonah color, but he said they did not talk about ghosts.

"If they ever come back, I hope they come back with the money," he said.

But if the Ringling ghosts are in Sarasota as many believe then there must be more ghosts than Toby the Cocker Spaniel.

With that thought in mind, I continued to interview circus people in search of the most elusive spirits in Sarasota — the spooks of the big top.

Retired circus performers live all around the area and when they die, they generally remain in the area. Most are laid to rest in cemeteries in Bradenton, Sarasota and Venice.

Karl Wallenda, the great wire walker, was buried in Bradenton after his fatal fall while performing in Puerto

Kim Cool

Rico on March 22, 1978.

His sister, Jennie Wallenda said that many of the great circus animals are buried on the site of the former Sarasota winter home of the circus, a 200-acre plot of land that is now home to the Glen Oak Estate development. It is said that in the 1940s, more than 100,000 tourists used to visit Sarasota annually just to see the winter quarters of the circus. That site does have a mystical feeling about it.

Sarasota remains the home of Show Folk of America, the exclusive club for circus performers and fans.

I went there while researching circus stories for *Ghost Stories of Venice*, proving only what St. Clair said. "Circus performers are a superstitious lot" and they generally do not talk about ghosts.

Perhaps they would not be so reticent if they knew that their former circus priest from the the 1920s remains in Sarasota, dwelling in the shadows at Ca d'Zan, the former home of John and Mable Ringling.

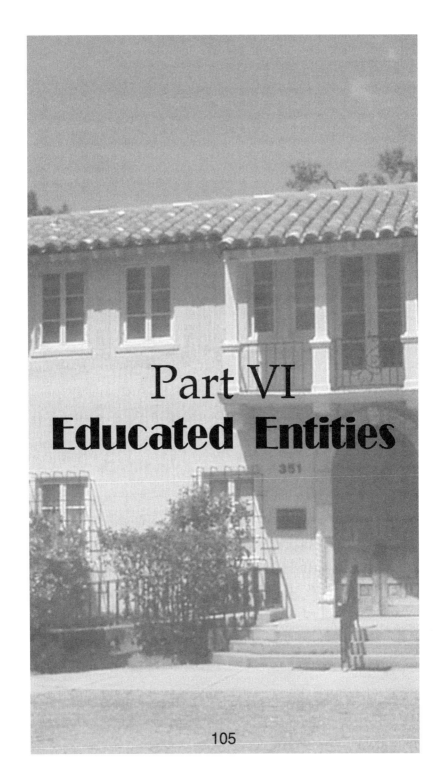

Part VI
Educated Entities

Kim Cool

Haunting prepper

It is only fitting that the oldest private school in Sarasota would have one of the town's oldest ghosts.

The school is the Out of Door Academy, founded in 1924 on Siesta Key as a progressive day and resident school for boys and girls aged 3-16. It is an independent, co-educational, college preparatory school. Towering banyan trees shelter the historic buildings of the old campus on Siesta Key.

Upper school students attend the school's new Lakewood Ranch campus which opened in 2001. It is east of Interstate 75.

The ghost, a former horse trainer, confines himself to the lower school campus. There, amidst the towering banyan trees that date to the school's earliest days, the male wraith can often be heard talking to his horses.

I could find no reports of the horses whinnying in return but I did find one person who said that he had heard the sound of a horse trotting along the street late at night and on more than one occasion.

When he looked out his window — there was nothing to be seen.

That is not the case with other scholarly ghosts in the Sarasota area, especially at the Ringling School of Art and Design where students regularly see signs of spectral activity.

Nor is it the case at New College where nocturnal activity in at least one building has become an almost nightly norm.

Kim Cool

In the still of the night

It seems that Sarasota County has a few poltergeists with a penchant for power — electrical power.

While writing "Ghost Stories of Venice," I learned about two such specters. One, a mischievous spook that repeatedly readjusted the electrically operated seats in his former car. He would push the buttons and move the seats whenever the car was driven by anyone other than his widow.

The other machine-savvy ghost in the Venice book was a cowboy ghost that spent an inordinate amount of time toying with the copy machines in a South County office complex late at night. Several people told me about him as I was writing that first book. They said he was dressed like a ranchhand might have dressed about 1950 or so. The land on which the office complex is located had once been part of the 15,000-acre Taylor Ranch, still a working ranch to this day.

Soon after that tale was in print, I learned that a new employee at the office park "met him." She had not read about him nor had she been told about the ghost before the night she had to work late. Thinking herself alone in the building, she was taken aback when she heard the distinct sound of the copy machine spewing out multiple copies. One of the reasons she was there that late was to have access to the machine without waiting. But who else was there that night?

Biding her time, she got her papers ready to be copied and was beginning to grow impatient with the other late-night worker when the sounds from the copy machine ceased. It was her turn at last.

Anxious to complete her tasks, she did not take notice of the fact that she had seen no one leave the copy area.

Setting the machine to automatically collate, making sure there was plenty of paper installed, the lady put the originals in place, pushed the button and went back to her

Kim Cool

desk to ready a second batch of papers for copying.

When the machine stopped, she returned, prepared to install a fresh stack of originals for the next job.

But when she got to the copy machine, something was wrong. Despite being correctly collated and stapled, every sheet of paper was the wrong color. All the copies had been printed on yellow paper!

Certain she had checked that there was plenty of white paper in the machine, she rechecked every paper drawer, ascertaining that the huge machine was indeed loaded with nothing but white paper.

Still, one of the drawers may have had just enough yellow paper for that first run.

Never assume.

This time she would not assume. She checked carefully and was certain she would have her white copies.

She reloaded the first set of originals, pushed the buttons, and headed back to her desk while the machine did its work.

Time was wasting and she still had much to do that night.

There was no other sound save the intermittent whirr of the machine and the gentle click of the collating function coupled with the *slap slap slap* as the originals were spewed out on the top of the machine.

Finally, the sounds ceased.

She returned to fetch her copies, positive that all would be right, and white.

But when she approached the machine, the only thing that was white was her face — ashen white.

Once again, all the copies were on yellow paper.

There was no visible explanation for what happened. She was certain she had checked every drawer.

Was her mind playing tricks on her or was someone or something else in the building, someone or something capable of changing the settings or switching the paper in the machine?

She had seen no one nor had she heard any sounds other than the mechanical sounds of the copy machine.

And then she saw "him," walking down the hallway.

He was an older man, dressed in Levis, wearing a plaid shirt, sort of like an old ranch hand. He walked away from her, down the dimly lit corridor, vanishing at the end.

She would make no more copies that night.

The next day, she told her co-workers about the yellow copies and the strange man she had seen in the hallway.

"Oh, you met the cowboy," they said.

The cowboy of Taylor Ranch had returned yet again.

Kim Cool

In the north end of the county, a similar incident plays itself out almost daily — or, nightly to be more exact.

On the Sarasota campus of the University of South Florida is a beautiful old Italianate house from the 1920s. Now used as an administration building for the university, the house once belonged to Hester Ringling, the daughter of Charles and Edith Conway Ringling and the niece of John and Mable Ringling. It is located between Ca d'Zan (the John Ringling house) and the Charles Ringling home, along Sarasota Bay on university property.

Hester was born in 1893, the year of the World's Fair in Chicago, where fan dancer Sally Rand regaled audiences as the Ringling circus was beginning to prosper in Baraboo, Wisconsin. Young Hester traveled in her family's private railroad car each summer as the Greatest Show on Earth criss-crossed the country.

In her biography, penned by her daughter-in-law, Alice Lancaster, Hester was described as being gifted with both intelligence and a "sixth sense." The latter was vigorously discouraged by her parents. The Ringlings were just doing what so many parents do when their children speak of seeing people or other creatures unseen and not understood by the elders. By the age of 10 or so, given enough discouragement, those imaginary friends tend to disappear. Several mediums I have spoken with say that their natural psychic abilities or "sixth sense" may also disappear at the same time. In the case of Hester, the young girl may have simply put her sixth sense on the back burner, waiting for another time.

As an adult, Hester married three times, raised two sons, was an actress at the Players Theatre in Sarasota, a voice coach and a playwright, all while living in her elegant waterfront home, now known as Cook Hall. Her brother Robert, a gifted baritone, died in 1950. His cottage, to the north of the parents' home, also has been deeded to the college. Hester died in 1965.

The spirit of Hester Ringling Parks Lancaster Sanford, the actress/playwright, may remain in Cook Hall.

Late at night, on many nights, the sound of a copy machine emanates from the building. Night watchmen have seen lights coming from the copy machines, even when the machines have been unplugged.

There have been no reports of a cowboy.

Instead, there have been reports of a lady seen staring from an upstairs window, both in broad daylight and at dusk. The room in which she appears was once a bedroom or an upstairs sitting room. Today, the room houses only file cabinets and computer servers. No one, man or woman, works in that room on any kind of regular schedule, according to information gathered from two people who work at the university. Nor does anyone work regularly in that building in the evening when the copy machines mysteriously whirr and hum, all on their own.

Does Hester run those machines at night? Is she writing a sequel to "Pearls and Sawdust," her play that was performed at The Players.

Or are the machines being run by her uncle John who lived next door at Ca d'Zan (House of John). John's presence also has been sensed by more than one person on more than one occasion.

John was quite a technophile for his time, employing state of the art mechanical devices in his house. Ca d'Zan had one of the first elevators in Sarasota and a sophisticated electrical system for its day. John certainly would have enjoyed the use of a copy machine to assist him in his voluminous paperwork.

His spirit is said to have appeared several times in the area of his former office, appearing to be disgruntled because his revolving bookcase is no longer there.

Or, are the machines being run by Mable Ringling in an attempt to replace her personal papers, papers that disappeared after her death.

Ca d'Zan reopened to the public in 2002 after a multi-million dollar renovation. The Otis elevator is operational once more and every bit of wiring and plumbing has been replaced. Air conditioning and state of the art humidity systems have been installed to protect the building and its contents in its new life as a museum adjunct. There is even an Australian-designed smoke detector system that itself is nearly undetectable to the casual observer. If you spot a dime-sized implant in the wall of a room, that is the detector which is capable of discerning the striking of a match even outside the room, giving ample time to warn occupants of any potential hazard.

While mechanical things were updated, glass and plaster and other physical components of the mansion were replaced.

Thanks to an extensive paper trail leading back to the home's construction in the late 1920s, many of these replacements came from the original manufacturers.

Broken panes of window glass in the first floor great room were replaced with new colored glass made by the same company in Chicago that had supplied the original glass. Gilding of the trim in the main rooms was repaired by workers from the firm that had done the original work. Edison stucco was used to repair the home's terra cotta surface. The original stucco formulas were created by Ringling's friend, inventor Thomas Alva Edison, who also wintered in South Florida. New stucco came from Edison Coatings in Plainsville, Conn. The historical accuracy of the restoration work was possible because there was a paper trail from John, his architect and his builder.

There was no such paper trail for any of the decorative work ordered by Mable. Had there been a copy machine, perhaps some information would have survived. Instead, there is not one piece of paper that bears her handwriting, not one piece of paper that bears her signature, according to Aaron DeGroft, the director of the John and Mable Ringling Museum of Art.

Mable died shortly after she and John moved into the house and all her papers vanished. John himself died a few years later and while he had changed his will, leaving just $5,000 to his sister Ida, he had not changed his executor. Ida and her son John Ringling North were named the executors of the Ringling estate. Because Mable had predeceased John, any of her remaining papers would have become part of her husband's estate.

Whether Mable's papers were simply thrown out by

heirs, lawyers or disgruntled executors during the probate process is of little consequence. The damage was done long ago. What does matter is that not one single piece of paper containing Mable's handwriting remains.

Maybe Hester does not run those copy machines after all. Perhaps it is the spirit of Mable, trying to right a wrong, to replace the lost papers.

For my money, that is a more plausible thought.

In my research, everything I could learn about Mable pointed to her as a person who would have left detailed records of her work. DeGroft said that she did not hire a decorator to help her with the house, instead making the decisions on her own, or with John. It is known that they bought furniture at auction from the Astor estate and the source of the wooden Venetian blinds was found during the home's recent renovation but so much is missing.

If Mable is in fact running the machines, perhaps one day she will learn to reproduce some of the missing papers. As technology advances one might assume that there would be an advancement in the way spirits send their messages from the beyond.

Never assume.

Well, maybe just this once.

Kim Cool

New College, Old Ghost

Anne Cederberg shared another story of a collegiate ghost.

This tale was passed on to her by a professor friend at New College, a liberal arts school located on 140 bayfront acres south of the Ringling Museum complex.

New College was founded in 1960 as a private college for academically gifted students. In 1975 it became part of the State of Florida system following a merger with the University of South Florida. It is the state's independent honors college and has been named one of the best bargains in higher education in such magazines as "Business Week" and "Money." Part of the New

College campus was originally the Caples Estate, the smallest estate in the museum area. It belonged to Ralph Caples and his wife Ellen.

The ghost is thought to be that of Ralph who had been a city passenger agent for the Delaware, Lackawanna and Western Railroad Company when he arrived in Sarasota in 1899 with his bride. He liked the city and recognized the potential the city would have should railroad lines be extended south from Tampa.

By 1909, both he and Sarasota were on their way financially and he built the Caples Building in downtown Sarasota. He continued to acquire additional land in the area and to promote the young resort town. It was Caples, with his friend Charles N. Thompson, who persuaded John and Charles Ringling to come to Sarasota. The year was 1911.

The Caples had purchased their residence on nearby Shell Beach in 1909.

Ralph Caples died in 1949 but his wife Ellen continued to live on the estate until her death in 1971 when the property was deeded to New College. The adjacent Ringling estate eventually became part of the University of South Florida so that even in death, there remains a connection between the Caples and the Ringlings.

Just as there are numerous reports of sightings of the

Kim Cool

ghost of John Ringling, there are reports at New College of sightings of the ghost of Ralph Caples, especially late at night when all is still.

"There is movement in the halls," Anne said. "And in the middle of the night, there often is the sound of a piano playing.

"One night, the campus police heard the piano playing and decided to check. There was no one there.

"The piano seems to play itself."

And there may be one other ghost in the former Caples house, a ghost who resembles Anne's friend, the professor.

"A woman student was walking by the former home one night," Anne said. "She saw a man on the balcony and he asked her why she was there.

"He looked just like my friend, the professor, but my friend had not been there."

All stirred up

Sarasota's legacy as the arts capital of Florida is directly attributed to John Ringling.

So too are several ghosts that are said to have what might be called a colorful past.

During the Florida land boom of the 1920s, Ringling decided he needed a hook to make people choose Sarasota over any other city in Florida. It was his idea that the arts would be that hook. To that end he set out to build the John and Mable Ringling Museum of Art adjacent to his terra cotta mansion Ca d'Zan, along Sarasota Bay.

Shortly thereafter, he set the wheels in motion to

establish the Ringling School of Art. It opened in 1931, just south of his museum.

 Unlike the museum, which was built on bare ground, the school was built on the site of the former Bay Haven Hotel and that building was transformed into dormitory space for out-of-town students. In the ensuing years, a number of students have witnessed several unexplained occurrences and visitations.

Several students have reported seeing a paint brush stirring water in a glass when no one was present to be holding the brush. At least one student has reported having seen objects levitate for a few seconds before falling back to a table top, and several students have reported seeing the shadowy figure of a young lady.

For many years, that female specter seemed to be the only ghost of the school. She alone received all the credit for the many strange occurrences.

I think she has company.

In talking with past and present students I learned that there were two unfortunate deaths on the campus. Both involved young ladies. Both were suicides. They occurred some 40 years apart.

The first occurred just before the school was founded, when the Bay Haven was still being operated as a hotel.

It took just four years for the hotel to go from boom

to bust.

As business declined with the onset of the Great Depression and the end of the Florida land boom of the 1920s, the hotel's clientele changed, and the hotel earned a seedier reputation before finally closing its doors about 1930. The Bay Haven had only been in business for four years yet it did not close soon enough for one young lady of the evening. She was known only

Photo by Kim Cool

Built as the Bay Haven Hotel, the present Keating Center was the first building to house students of the Ringling School of Art and Design.

by her first name, Belle.

The facts about Belle are somewhat sketchy. Even her name has been changed over the years as her story has been told and retold. Nowadays she is more commonly known as Mary.

By whatever name, Belle, or Mary, became despondent, deciding to end her life by her own hand about 1929.

She was found hanging in a third-floor staircase at the hotel.

Fearful that the news of her suicide would not be good for what little business remained, someone at the hotel decided to keep the story out of the papers and hide the body.

The cover-up may have gone undiscovered for years had it not been for the hotel's closing and subsequent purchase as another cog in the Ringling plan to make Sarasota an important center for the arts.

Within months of the sale, work began to transform the hotel into dormitory space for the new college.

When the construction workers arrived to begin the renovation of hotel rooms to dorm rooms for the new art school, they made the grisly discovery. They found a skeleton, thought to be that of Belle, in the boarded up staircase area where she had died.

Ghost Stories of Sarasota

To this day that area is unused, off limits to students. Whatever has been done to that staircase over the years, it never deterred Belle's ghost from making occasional appearances.

The second suicide occurred in 1977 according to information told to me by Tim Jaeger, a Ringling graduate who was working at Sarasota News & Books on the day we talked about the ghosts of the Ringling School.

"I was a teaching assistant at Ringling," he said. "One day I heard a scream. It was very early in the morning. A lady cleaning the bathroom had seen a reflection in the mirror but there was no one there.

"She quit right then and there. These people do not just quit their jobs and she needed the money but she had definitely seen something."

Did she see Belle or did she see the ghost of another lady? She did not stay around long enough to tell anyone.

Jaeger continued with his tale, speaking of room 210, the room in which the second suicide occurred.

"People who lived in that room would levitate above their beds while asleep," he said. "No one was ever hurt."

Though unhurt, they usually requested to be moved from the room, he continued. He had been told the story

125

by his girlfriend's roommate who had lived in an adjacent room in 1978. She too asked to be moved.

The building has been transformed yet again. Now called the Keating Center, the building now serves as an administration building for the college.

Other cleaning ladies have seen ghostly images and similar unexplained sights in the ladies rest room, so often that it has become standard practice by many of them to prop the door open while they are working.

Despite such precautions, one night a cleaning lady was tapped on the shoulder by a shadowy figure holding one finger to her lips as if to say, "shhh." When the mystery lady vanished through a door that had not been propped open, the cleaning lady very nearly did the same. Legend has it that, like the lady in Jaeger's story, that particular cleaning lady never returned.

A third female specter is associated with those stirring tales of paintbrushes. She is reported to have been seen walking the second floor corridors late at night. On the nights when she is reported to have been seen in the corridors, it is said that as the art students return to their rooms they find swirling paintbrushes in their watercolor rinse cups. The identity of this female specter remains unknown but it could be a deceased student who simply wants to continue her studies.

And then, there is the incident that can best be described as a fashion statement.

It happened after Christmas vacation, back in the late 1940s. The story was related to me by Anne Cederberg who lives a few blocks away in the Indian Beach neighborhood, one of the ghostliest areas of Sarasota. She has been researching Sarasota ghosts for some time and has several intriguing stories that date to the early days of the city by the bay.

This tale involved an art student from the north who was heading home for the Christmas holidays, never realizing that she would receive an extra present on her return.

"The student closed and locked her closet and then locked the door to her dorm room before leaving for vacation," Cederberg said. "When she returned a few weeks later, something was amiss."

The student unlocked her dorm room only to find that her closet was no longer locked as it had been when she left for vacation.

In fact, the closet door was slightly ajar.

Opening it further, she noticed that her clothing had been moved.

Someone or something had moved all her clothing to either side of the closet. The same thing had been done to her shoes. They were all lined up on either side of the closet floor, with a space between them.

In the void at the center of the closet there hung one lacy dress, a dress that would have been worn in the late1920s.

Directly below the dress was a pair of silk shoes in a color that was a perfect match for the dress.

Belle was nowhere in sight but the student who made the discovery was convinced that the dress and shoes had been worn by that earlier visitor to the hotel, Cederberg said.

Part VII
Graveyard Shift

Kim Cool

Graven images

Rosemary Cemetery is the oldest cemetery in Sarasota. It does not appear to be the oldest haunted site in the city. It may not be haunted at all.

That should come as no surprise for more ghosts have been experienced in places other than cemeteries. Why haunt a cemetery when there are interesting theaters, old hotels, historic homes and other places where many more things have happened?

So, while the bodies of the city's first mayors and early settlers may be buried at Rosemary Cemetery, the city's more artistically inclined spirits are more likely to be found in the area's many theaters, its historic neighborhoods and especially in the city's most famous house, Ca d'Zan, the former home of John and Mable Ringling.

What does haunt the historic cemetery is a sense of pride that keeps the living coming back to clean up the two-acre plot of land that was established as a burial ground in 1886, deeded to the city in 1903 and put under the protection of the then newly formed Rosemary Cemetery Committee in 1985.

Still reposing there is the first customer, Tom Booth, who was buried in 1887.

During 2002, an independent study project was conducted under the leadership of New College Professor Uzi Baram and eight students. They completed a survey of the site, grave markers and recorded the condition of vaults and markers, making drawings of them.

Should urban development lead to the displacement of the cemetery's present dwellers, perhaps a true ghost story or two may emerge. Until then, peace seems to reign over, and under, this hallowed ground located just seven blocks from the heart of downtown Sarasota.

The cemetery is open for visitors daily.

At night ... well, at night, it may be open to others.

Part VIII
Ringlings & Friends

Home again

The ghosts of John and Mable Ringling have reason to smile again.

Ca d'Zan, their former Sarasota winter home on Sarasota Bay, has been fully restored to its former grandeur after a $15 million, six-year project. Said to have been inspired by the Doge's palace in Venice, Italy, as well as by several Tuscan villas, the 22,000-square-foot, 32-room mansion reopened to the public in late April 2002, during the city's centennial year. It had been built in 1926 at a cost of $1.5 million.

The restoration work happened just in time. Water damage, time and the elements and a steady stream of visitors were taking their toll. Windows were broken. Plumbing was in disrepair. Plaster was crumbling and so was some of the terra cotta trim on the building's exterior.

The dock has seen better times but the waterfront site selected by John Ringling is even more magnificent today than it was in 1925 when work began on the house. Breathtaking views of the water and Longboat Key just across the bay are upstaged nearly every evening by magnificent sunsets. It is no wonder that Mable's spirit is said to be drawn to the terrace of the terra cotta trimmed Italianate mansion that she occupied for just three years. Even John Ringling lived there less than 10 years before his passing.

Yet there is little doubt that their spirits remain.

Many visitors say there is a spirit that envelops the whole property. Employees also attest to that feeling.

"In certain parts of the property it is like time has not changed," Sarasota artist Rilla Fleming said. "There's a spirit there."

Rilla mans the cafe of Ca d'Zan, under the tent at the south end of the house, Tuesday-Friday, from 9 a.m.-4:30 p.m.

"On the back steps by the cafe, it feels like John Ringling is here sometimes," she said. "I know he gets upset sometimes. I feel like I want to speak for him but I can't."

She went on to say that she has felt the spirits of both John and Mable at several places on the property, but she also has felt other spirits.

"Between the circus museum and the caretaker's cottage, there is a graveyard of statues," Rilla said. "If you walked the old servants' road you would see it. I think in that area it (the feeling of spirits) is very strong. Maybe it is the age of the things there."

She said there are many broken statues, pieces of trim work and the like, placed there over the past 50 years or so. When the area was fenced off so that no one but museum personnel could go there, she noticed a change in the feelings she had in that area.

"I felt like those things should not have been fenced off," Rilla said of the area that is still visible beyond the new fencing.

The graveyard of statues is near another graveyard, the one holding the graves of John and Mable. Originally stored in New Jersey, their bodies were brought back to their winter home for burial a few years ago. Ca d'Zan "keeper" Ronald McCarty said.

"They are buried in a secret place."

While Ringling had traveled the country and even the world with his circus, he invested millions in

Kim Cool

Sarasota's waterfront property, developing nearby St. Armands CIrcle, Bird Key and Lido Key. When he built the John and Mable Ringling Museum of Art and acquired the museum's collection he guaranteed his own immortality even as he set in motion Sarasota's future as the culture capital of Florida.

Aaron DeGroft, chief curator of the Ringling museum, wrote his doctoral dissertation on John Ringling. According to DeGroft, Mable Ringling took many pictures of palaces and villas in Italy during the couple's travels. When they were planning Ca d'Zan, she dumped the piles of photos and many magazine clippings out on a table for the architect to study.

As the three-year project progressed from 1925-27, the Ringlings bought furniture at auction that had belonged to the Astors and even acquired whole rooms from historic mansions which they eventually had rebuilt within their own mansion or in the museum which they built later, DeGroft said.

Mable supervised much of the interior design although they both had a hand in the home's architecture and interior design. Unfortunately, any paperwork attributable to Mable disappeared shortly after her death in 1929 at the age of 54, DeGroft said.

What did remain are four photo albums. Those

albums proved invaluable during the recent renovations and restoration. The information that McCarty had gained from those photos also proved valuable on Feb. 4, 2003, when I toured the magnificent mansion with two mediums and a television crew from the Sarasota ABC channel.

I had been in Ca d'Zan when it was nearly at its worst in the early 1990s. It had suffered nearly all the

Photo by Kim Cool

Artist Rilla Fleming, an employee of the John and Mable Ringling home, Ca d'Zan, can tell when the spirits of John and Mable Ringling are happy or not.

indignities a building could stand from years of neglect.

I was there again on the day in April 2002 when the keys were returned from the renovators to the caretakers, the staff of the John and Mable Ringling Museum of Art.

That sunny April day, the house was empty, save the old Aolian organ that was built into the main reception room. Every surface sparkled. Broken window panes had been replaced with glass from the same Chicago company that had made the original. The gold leaf had been cleaned. Matching gold leaf had been applied where needed. All new mechanical systems had been installed. Plasterwork had been repaired on the interior and the terra cotta trimming on the home's exterior had been repaired or replaced as needed. Everything had been given a fresh coat of paint, including decorative painting and faux finishes, all according to those photos of Mable's.

Ca d'Zan was even more wonderful than it had been on the day that John and Mable had first moved in back in 1927.

Somehow I knew that if their spirits had ever left that place, they would now return.

It was that month when I first asked if I could return one evening with two mediums in search of the spirits of John and Mable.

There certainly were plenty of stories that suggested their spirits were there.

Yet the timing was not right in April 2002.

Perhaps the spirits of John and Mable wanted to make sure everything was perfect, as they had for their earlier guests back in 1927-29, the years when they entertained visiting heads of state, show business legends, circus people, real estate magnates and others.

John may have worn plain brown suits, but each had his name hand-embroidered within and the house in which the Ringlings lived was truly a gilded lily. One example is the gilded coffered ceiling of the ballroom, which featured hand-painted scenes. Another is the third floor game room decorated with fanciful caricatures by Hollywood set decorator Willy Pogeny,

John married once more, 18 months after Mable died, but was never so happy as he was with Mable. The young socialite who was his second wife never even occupied Mable's room, so attached was he to his first wife. John died of pneumonia in 1936.

When he died, he owned little more than Ca d'Zan, which he wished to bequeath to the state of Florida.

Though the Ringlings had no children, their nieces, nephews and others managed to tie up the settlement of the estate for some 10 years.

During that time, the house sat nearly empty and many of its furnishings were sold off. If the Ringling spirits remained during those years, their tears may have contributed to the water damage to the house.

Even after things were settled, the endowment left by Ringling lanquished, growing to just $1.8 million by 2000. Since being turned over to Florida State University that year, it has grown to $4 million, yet another reason for the Ringlings to smile again.

"You can tell when he is happy," Rilla said. "The whole place is happy and you think John is happy today and spreading his joy."

But John is not always happy, she said. Nor is Mable.

Rilla said that the museum has started to allow the serving of red wine at parties in the Rubens room of the museum and that John is very upset about that.

"It's his original wood floor that would be damaged by the wine," she said. "They also allow red wine to be served on the marble floored loggia surrounding the museum's courtyard and she thinks John is not pleased about that either.

Mable's ghost also has expressed her displeasure, Rilla said.

Shortly after the Terrorist Attack of Sept. 11, 2001, the entrance gates to the road that leads to Ca d'Zan were closed and locked. The gates have remained locked since that fateful day.

"That upset Mable," Rilla said. "The whole joy of coming to Ca d'Zan was driving the drive that John and Mable drove. Actually they both got upset. There was a heavy sadness because of that."

Rilla has had several psychic experiences. She spoke of the time her grandmother died and there was a mist in the room for three days. On the third day, that mist appeared at the foot of Rilla's bed. Sensing that is was the spirit of her grandmother and that perhaps her grandmother did not know what to do, she said, "Go to Jesus, Grandma." As she uttered the words, the mist vanished. She is sure that is when her grandmother crossed over to the other side.

When her step father died, Rilla had a different experience, more of an out of body experience.

"I think I was with him when he went to heaven," she said. "It was a beautiful room. I think I may have been in his coffin with him and when the top opened, there was this beautiful bright light and he went up into it like a vacuum. He said he loved me. I believe I experienced his spiritual ascension to God."

Those experiences have led her to develop some theories about ghosts and specters, especially the Ringling ghosts.

"They were eccentric and extravagant people," she said. "I think that the most eccentric and extravagant people are the strongest spirits. They are never satisfied so they are still searching."

As for the other spirits at Ca d'Zan, Rilla is not sure who they are but she has painted at least seven of them.

"I painted one of the banyan trees at Ca d'Zan," she said. "People who looked at the painting found seven people in the painting. I did not intend to paint those people."

She said that has happened in other paintings also, as if something is guiding her hand as she paints.

Rilla also shared one other tidbit about Ca d'Zan and John Ringling.

There is a watchman by the name of Mel who she said looks like John Ringling, portly but not very tall.

"He'll walk by sometimes and people will think they have seen John," she said. "They haven't. It was Mel."

Or was it? After all. Rilla is not the only one who has seen the ghost of John Ringling. On Feb. 4, 2003, several of us sensed even more than that.

Read on.

Ringling's last hurrah

Finally, the timing was right.

In December 2002, Ringling publicist Jeanne Lambert and Ringling marketing chief Carol Harwood decreed that I could visit Ca d'Zan with my friends Pat Charnley and Carol Lee.

Pat Charnley is the minister and founder of the Angel Ministries, a metaphysical church, in Venice. Carol Lee is director of the church's healing program, a certified healing touch therapist and artist. Both are mediums.

Charnley, from England, has been gifted with the ability to see spirits her entire life. Carol Lee has discovered her gifts only within the last few years.

The visit to Ca d'Zan was set for Tuesday, Feb. 4, 2003. We would be accompanied by Harwood; the Keeper of Ca d'Zan, Ron McCarty; WWSB anchorwoman Vida Urbonas and her photo journalist, Albert Im, from the ABC Channel 40 affiliate in Sarasota.

Allowing plenty of time for the heavy seasonal traffic in Florida, the two mediums and I arrived well before 6 p.m., just as the sun was beginning to set.

Harwood met us at the security entrance and led the way to the mansion via the back road that is used only be employees and the handicapped who need to be driven to the house which is located at the back of the extensive Ringling compound, on Sarasota Bay.

Evening was enveloping us as we got out of our cars and were led around to the back of the house. We passed beneath a giant banyan tree. It was the very one which had been painted by Rilla, the one in which people saw faces in the completed painting.

Perhaps the mediums would see some of those faces this night. Neither Pat Charnley nor Carol Lee had physically set foot in that house until that evening.

Entering the house from the former servants' entrance we found ourselves in what is now the gift shop. It had been the home's spacious kitchen. Still

there are the sinks and the built-in freezers and refriger-
ators, something unique back in the 1920s.

En route from Venice, Charnley had been thinking
ahead to the visit, actually mentally going into the
house. She had been doing that on and off for some
weeks she had said.

The two mediums work differently, and they were
not always in each room we visited at the same time, yet
they both touched in on many of the same spirits on a
night that was unlike any night that I had ever experienced.

By the time we left, there would be no doubt in anyone's mind that Ca d'Zan is indeed haunted.

Charnley touched in with the spirit of Mable immediately.

"That piece of furniture does not belong there,"
Charnley said as we passed through a small hallway
while walking toward the Tap Room.
"Those glass dishes do not belong there either."

She was referring to a buffet against the right wall on
which were two large blown glass objects. Imagine two
old-fashioned champagne glasses, not flutes, of spotted
blue glass, but nearly nine inches in diameter.

"You are right," an amazed Ron McCarty said.
"Those were not there when the Ringlings lived there.
"We put them there because they were of the period."

"Mable said that piece is all right," Charnley said as

she pointed to a telephone stand to the left. A two-piece telephone, circa 1929, was atop the stand.

Again McCarty concurred, saying that the telephone stand had been in the house when the Ringlings lived there.

With the spirit of Mable by our side, we progressed into the Tap Room.

Containing a built-in bar with a burled walnut edge on which to lean and lighted stained glass windows at the back, this room was the scene of many Ringling gatherings.

Photo by Kim Cool

On Feb. 4, 2003, the Tap Room at Ca d'Zan was filled with spirits seeking help in crossing over, according to the two mediums present that evening.

On that Tuesday night, it was to be the final party for the spirits of what may have been several hundred former Ringling friends, visitors, workers, circus performers and others.

As we entered the room, we felt a chill. This was not a chill caused from an air conditioning outlet. Ca d'Zan's new mechanical systems are of such quality as to provide uniform temperature and humidity throughout the house.

"That chill is the spirits guiding us to our work," Carol Lee said. "One by one we will call in their energy and you will feel the difference as the energy shifts.

Our speech will change and our personalities will change as we connect with the spirits."

There were many spirits gathered in the room that night.

When asked how many, both mediums laughed, explaining that spirits do not take up a lot of room and there could be untold numbers of them there. Consider that this room is possibly no more than 14 by 20 feet in size.

"They said that things are not the same," Carol Lee continued.

Charnley said the spirited guests were all dressed in different ways, many in costumes, some in workers' clothing and one, a man, dressed in black with a black hat. As she described this one man in particular it seemed that she might be describing the spirit of the circus priest who traveled on the train with the show. To this day, a priest or other clergyman accompanies the show from city to city during the season.

The two mediums said that these spirits had gathered for one last hurrah at the mansion before "crossing over," something that the mediums would facilitate that evening and that when that happened, the room would no longer be so cold.

"I have spoken to them all and they are preparing to go," Charnley said. "They set this up, by the way."

Charnley was referring to the timing of our visit. She knew I had asked for the visit in April and at that time had said it would happen when the timing was right.

As we left the Tap Room Urbonas and Im arrived. From that point on, for nearly three hours, as we moved from room to room throughout the house, Im taped and Urbonas asked questions, took notes or simply watched and felt what was happening in that house that night.

Charnley walked into the formal dining room, immediately sensing the spirit of John Ringling.

"He is seated over there, smoking a cigar," she said.

McCarty looked nearly ashen, saying that he had just put some of John Ringling's cigars on display in the room earlier that day.

"Right as she said that, I felt a chill on my arm,"

McArty said. "It was right where she said it would be."

"John and Mable are both here," Charnley said. "They would not be here if they didn't approve."

The ornate, heavily paneled room with coffered ceiling is one of the most elegant rooms in the house, holding a banquet table that can easily seat 20 or more for a formal dinner. A hand-made carpet is on the floor.

Charnley continued through the dining room into the main living area of the house, the entrance area through which visitors normally enter the house. She paused, looked around, trying to find something in particular.

At least three weeks before we visited the house, Charnley had remarked to me about a dream in which she had seen a curved staircase and a picture.

"There it is," she said. "That is the picture I saw."

And just through the doorway next to the picture was the curving staircase leading to the upper floors.

In her dream she thought she had seen a man on horseback but the picture was small and not clear. In the house there was a large painting on the wall above a table. On the table was a black and white photo of the painting, the doorway and the staircase. The photo was taken in the late 1920s and to my eyes did resemble a man on horseback when viewed from some distance. It was the photo that Charnley had envisioned, not the actual painting. The painting was of a woman in the ornate dress of a noble person of the 18th century or earlier. It was very dark.

As the camera rolled we climbed the marble stairs, one by one, holding on to the carved marble railing on the right hand wall.

At the top of the stairs we went into John's bedroom. Although handsomely furnished with gold-leaf decorated twin sleigh beds and hand-loomed carpets, it was not the furniture that would stun us that night.

"There are two little girls playing in this room," Charnley said.

"Mable used to take care of her niece and two nephews," McCarty said. Perhaps the young niece had acquired a new friend as a spirit.

Next, Charnley sensed the spirit of John's manservant.

While Carole Lee walked into Mable's room, Charnley, McCarty and the TV crew headed into the servants' wing.

Those rooms are not ever open to the public, used now instead as offices and small conference rooms.

Charnley said the manservant had been very happy in that house and had returned because he wanted to continue to care for the house and his master's objects. Also in that area of the house was the spirit of a maid.

"It is a female spirit," Charnley said. "She was disgraced and dismissed by the Ringlings but she liked the house and has come back."

Like the spirits in the Tap Room, this female spirit would not remain but would be helped to cross over, Charnley said.

"Can you feel the breeze," she asked. "Everything is energy and the higher the frequency when they make the transition, the colder.

"Your grandmother (Harwood's grandmother) is here and so is Kim's husband.

"I literally have to make them back off. We literally have 100 different energies running in and out when we are doing this. We are guided to this."

In Mable's room, Carol Lee had discovered a big fluffy gray cat.

"There used to be a cat that slept in this bed," she said.

McCarty and Howard both said that Mable had a lot of animals and while they did not know if one was a big fluffy gray cat, they agreed that the animal spirit might have been that of her cat.

"I sense a lot of peace and love in this room," Charnley said. "a woman who stays here a lot."

"Everything in this room is identical to what was in the photos," McCarty said. "John always protected this space."

"She doesn't like these here," Pat said, pointing to the red roping that keeps visitors from walking into all corners of the room. (On the night of our visit, we were allowed to ignore such ropes and barriers.)

"She said it has been wonderful to watch you do this work (on the house)," Charnley said to McCarty. "She loves your energy."

Approaching the settee in one corner, Charnley spoke of Mable's private maid, "a pretty little thing"

{photo by Kim Cool

Ghostly shadows and orbs appeared in this one photo taken in the former bedroom of Mable Ringling. Note the ghostly shadows on the left rear wall and another on the settee.

who used to sit and do her hair here."

McCarty said that everything in the room had been Mable's although a few items might have been arranged a bit differently.

Going toward Mable's dressing room, Charnley said that Mable spoke of how cold the room had often been when she was changing clothes and that it was a little warmer these days.

In the 1920s the house was not air conditioned and since it is located right on the water, it could well have

Photo by Kim Cool
ABC photo journalist Albert Im, at right, films Ca d'Zan curator Ron McCarty and Pat Charnley, minister of the Church of the Angels in Venice. The setting is the bath/dressing room of Mable Ringling.

Kim Cool

been quite chilly and damp in the evening.

The floor of her dressing room is marble, a substance which would remain cool even on the warmest Florida day.

As McCarty pointed out Mable's actual linens, Im focused in on a closeup shot for the TV segment. Carole Lee continued to speak of the big fluffy gray cat, wandering about with us.

"She felt very close to that cat," Carole Lee said.

Charnley said the dressing room area felt very sacred.

"He was a great protector of her," McCarty said of

Photo by Kim Cool

Orbs like those in this photo appeared in five of the more than 20 photos taken at Ca d'Zan on Feb. 4, 2003. Mediums, Carol Lee and Pat Charnley, above, say the orbs are "angels."

John Ringling.

Charnley again sensed the spirits of two little girls, saying their initials were J and M and that Mable loved them dearly. Walking through the next room, the mediums and the TV folks stepped out onto the balcony overlooking the living room below.

Photo by Kim Cool

Mediums, Carol Lee and Pat Charnley, above, on the balcony overlooking Ca d'Zan's great room, accompanied, they said, by the ghost of John Ringling.

"John is here, overlooking the balcony," Carole Lee said. "The energy is with us. It is warm here. That is his presence.

I am very hot."

At this point, McCarty opened one of the albums he had been carrying, to show a rare photo of Mable. Like her jewelry and clothing that was taken by her relatives when she died, there are few photos and no paper remaining from her existence in the house.

"The pictures of the children will come to you," Carole Lee said to McCarty.

As they spoke, I took several digital photos of the mediums on the balcony. One, included with this tale is filled with many unexplainable dots. Are they spirits? Some would say so.

Halfway through the house, it was now time to go the third and fourth floors, areas that are off limits to the public because there is just one staircase. Local fire laws do not allow public access to such areas.

We had already experienced chills and heavy pressure on our chests on the first and second floors.

What might we find on the upper floors, especially in the legendary third floor game room?

Behind the locked gate

Ron McCarty pulled out the ring of Ca d'Zan keys.

We were about to go to the most private areas of the Ringling mansion, the areas that are off limits to casual visitors and the areas that have generated the most speculation among amateur ghost hunters.

As the keeper of Ca d'Zan unlocked the massive gate that closes off the marble staircase to the upper two floors of the house, the local ABC TV cameraman, Albert Im, zoomed in for a close-up of the lock. There was a sense of excitement in the air.

"There is a very mixed energy here," Reverend Pat

Kim Cool

Charnley said.

"There was a shift in energy," Carole Lee concurred.

After climbing the spiral staircase to the third floor, we paused, waiting for Im to catch up with us. We stood before the "playroom."

"It is almost like you cannot breathe," Charnley said as she entered the room. "Someone passed over in here."

One by one, as we entered the space, we each felt a heaviness weighing on our chest and a very cold spot just inside the door.

It was almost as though we were each having the beginnings of a heart attack.

Fortunately the feeling went away once we were inside the room. The mediums had said earlier that they had sent a message to the spirits to allow us to sense them and perhaps even to see them. In this room, even more than in the Tap Room, it was as though they had indeed received that message and, more importantly, had agreed to act on it.

"I do not feel any female energy in here," Charnley said.

"I feel that someone passed over in that doorway," Carol Lee said.

And then she said something that surprised all of us because she was picking up the spirit of someone who had worked for the circus but not until some 25 or 30 years after John Ringling had died.

"I am picking up Gunther," she said. (Gunther Gebel-Williams, the legendary animal trainer had died in Venice in July 2001, at the age of 66. He was famous for the way in which he revolutionized the treatment of animals in the circus, using love rather than whips.)

"One of his cats has fallen and injured its C-3 disk," she continued, "and one of his elephants has a problem with his right front foot. He wants us to let someone know so they can help the animals."

A skeptic could say she just said that because everyone in Venice knows about Gebel-Williams' love of his animals but none of us could discount what Carol Lee said next.

"I feel the presence of Willy in this room," she said. "He is saying, 'I did the best I could for what I had to do. It tells a story and know that we had lots of fun and many secrets in this room but those secrets will stay here. Every design tells a story'."

Carol Lee said she had never been inside Ca d'Zan. She had never been in this room. There is virtually no way she could have known that a man by the name of Willy Pogeny had painted the caricatures that were all over the ceiling of the game room.

Entitled, "Carnival in Venice," the illustrations fea-

Kim Cool

tured the Ringlings and their friends, all in fanciful costumes, plus a self-portrait of Pogeny. It is the last portrait seen to the right as one exits the room.

Also pictured is John and Mable's German shepherd,

Photo by Kim Cool

Self-portrait of artist Willy Pogeny was the last of the caricatures painted by the artist in the John Ringling game room on the third floor of the Ringling mansion along the bay in Sarasota.

a cockatoo, a grey parrot and Manchester terriers. Support posts are painted to look like the colorful poles that edge the canals of Venice, Italy.

Turning to McCarty, Carol Lee said that Willy's family would soon share information about Willy and his paintings with the museum.

She also offered an explanation for the heavy feeling we all experienced, saying that the energy we felt could well have been his and that it is quite possible that he died of a heart attack, although not in that room.

McCarty said that Pogeny had died in 1955. I could not find the exact cause in any of several biographies of the artist but one said that he worked right up until his death and implied that his death was sudden. He was 73.

There were no other spirits present in the game room but the heavy pressure and the mention of Willy had been enough to convince even the most skeptical one in our group on the night of Feb. 4 that John and Mable's spirits were not alone in that great big house.

But there was more to come that special night.

It was time to head upstairs to the top floor, site of the Ringling's most special guest room. Located at the top of the house, this room offers incredible views up and down the coast of Sarasota Bay.

"I feel as if a president might have slept here," Carol

Lee said as she entered the room.

"I feel that this is a transient place, not totally connected to any one person or couple," Charnley said.

McCarty concurred that Charnley was correct that
this was a guest room and that many different people
had stayed here. He said that the Ringlings were friends
of several presidents but he did not know if any of them
ever had stayed in the house.

"One could have been here," McCarty said. "This is
the room in which the Ringlings housed their major guests."

"Probably two presidents stayed in that room,"
Carol Lee said as she stood next to a large chair in one
corner of the room.

When the Ringling Circus had played Washington,
D.C., John Ringling had personally escorted President
and Mrs. Coolidge to their seats.

"There also is a husband and wife here," she said.
"They were very close. He caressed her and he talked to
her about documents here."

McCarty suggested that the couple could be Flo
Ziegfeld and his wife Billy Burke who were frequent
guests in the house. He added that they did work close-
ly together.

"I feel a lot of money matters were discussed in this
room," Carol Lee said. "She (Billy Burke) is telling me

that John was a great businessman and that they were all able to make money."

The two mediums also got a sense of the spirit of Will Rogers. He too had been a frequent guest in the house.

It was time to head back downstairs. We had been in the house for two hours. The mediums had made contact with several hundred spirits and each of of us had had several experiences of our own.

Vida Urbonas, the local ABC anchor wanted to interview us for the TV spot and then she had to return to the station for the 11 p.m. newscast.

And the mediums still had a little work to do to ensure that all those spirits had indeed crossed over as they had wished.

Arriving back on the second floor, we waited while McCarty locked the gate once again.

While he did that he shared some of his experiences as the Keeper of Ca d'Zan for some 20 years.

"It was very much in need of attention," he said. "In the time I have been here, I have found things, and saved them. Every rug in the house had been rolled up and stored in the attic. I also found many of his personal documents and lots of things with her monogram."

We descended the final set of stairs, walked around the downstairs, admiring the needlework in the living

Kim Cool

room and the hand-painted ceiling in the ballroom before returning to the Tap Room.

As Urbonas interviewed McCarty, he repeated the story about feeling the cold energy on his arm as he passed by the arm chair where Pat Charnley had seen the spirit of John Ringling smoking a cigar.

"I felt the cold energy," he said. "As I did what she said, my arm was quite cold to the touch. She said he was smoking a cigar and I had just finished a display with one of his actual cigars."

The Tap Room was definitely warmer. All the spirits had gone, save one.

Photo by Kim Cool
A few spirits remain at Ca d'Zan, the former winter home of John and Mable Ringling.

The circus priest remained, seated on the sofa, the mediums said.

"He is at that end," they said. "If you put your hand there you will feel his presence. It will be warmer there."

We all put our hands in the area where they pointed and it was indeed warmer than the rest of the room.

"Kim, you are leaning on him," Carol Lee said to me.

I moved away, not wanting to dent a spirit.

Also choosing to stay in the house were the spirits of John and Mable.

"They have no desire to leave," Charnley said. "Mable used to have big parties on the terrace. Now she loves to dance on the terrace."

The mediums had two more things to do that night.

First, they said they put a white light over the entire building and a golden pyramid above it. Then they covered that with an angel's white veil to protect the house.

"From now on, if anyone with negative energy enters the house, the negative energy will remain outside," Charnley said.

Second, they had a message for McCarty from Mable.

"Mable is very pleased with what you have done for her house."

Before we left, I had one final question. In my research, I had come across stories of a "black marble room." We had been everywhere in that house but had not seen a black marble room. I asked McCarty about it. He opened one more door, on the first floor. It led into a restroom used by the home's docents and an occasional visitor. The room had a black floor but not marble. Other rooms had marble floors but none was black.

The solarium had a dark green marble floor but the room itself was bright and light, with two walls of windows. That certainly could never have been mistaken for a black marble room.

That story seemed to be just that - a story.

The stories about the ghosts of John and Mable were quite another thing.

On Feb. 4, 2003, Pat Charnley, Carol Lee, Carol Harwood, Vida Urbonas, Albert Im, Ron McCarty and I walked all through Ca d'Zan.

We were not alone.

Ca d'Zan calls her back

Less than a month after her first visit to Ca d'Zan, Medium Carol Lee returned with a medium named Rachel and Rilla Fleming, a local artist and part-time employee at Ca d'Zan. Like Carol Lee and Rachel, Fleming is gifted with psychic abilities.

Escorted by house curator Ron McCarty who had guided her through the house on Feb. 4 when we were filming a TV segment for the local ABC news show anchored by Vida Urbonas, Carol Lee discovered two rooms she had not seen on her first visit.

She also discovered another spirit, one she had not met on Feb. 4 — John Ringling's second wife.

"Emily lived in that house and she won't go away," Carol Lee said. "Her spirit is in a bedroom off to the side. We did not go into that room that night (Feb. 4)."

There are two guest bedrooms on the north side of the house, along the balcony that overlooks the great room below. Mable's bedroom, bath and dressing area was on the east side of the house, off the same balcony which wraps around the main living area on three sides. Mable's area has been preserved exactly as it was when she was alive and as it was during John Ringling's short marriage to his second wife.

"Emily's spirit was in the bedroom that was the farthest away from Mable's" Carol Lee continued. "When she entered the room, Rachel said something was not right.

"She went to the closet, opened the door and was literally bowled over with Emily's spirit."

Rachel talked to me later about the strong feelings that she had that day. She said that she sensed that Emily's departure from the house was not a happy one

Carol Lee said that on that return visit, she sensed a great many business deals that had been conducted in that house.

She also spoke of McCarty and his more than 20-year stint as curator of the house.

"I believe Ron is a spirit sent to the house to build its

reputation and to give it back to the community. He is spiritual, very gifted and very protective of the house."

Ideal qualities for the curator of the most famous house in Sarasota.

No wonder so many spirits refuse to leave the magnificent mansion on the bay.

Beyond the crypt

In the introduction to this book, I spoke of the charmed life I have been leading these past several months.

Perhaps that is why, in this second book of ghost stories, there are several photos which contain images of things that cannot be readily explained such as strange shadows or mysterious orbs.

On Feb. 4, 2003, when I entered Ca d'Zan in the company ot two mediums, a television crew and two Ringling employees, I expected to have an interesting evening. I was looking forward to seeing the lovely mansion dressed in all its finery after three years of renovations and reconstruction.

I expected that the mediums might sense the spirits of

Ghost Stories of Sarasota

John and Mable Ringling. That they would sense hundreds of spirits was as surprising to me as were the five of the pictures taken by me that evening. The mediums had said the spirits would allow themselves to be photographed. Perhaps that is explanation enough for these five photos.

But even more surprising than these stories and photos were two stories I never found.

There are more than a dozen stages in the greater Sarasota area. All but one were reported to have eerie sights and sounds. The one exception is the biggest auditorium of them all — the Van Wezel Performing Arts Hall, otherwise known as the "Purple People Seater." The city-owned facility annually plays host to the widest variety of entertainers of any area venue, hosting everything from string quartets and the Beach Boys to Broadway musicals, Bill Cosby and other comedians, magicians, movie stars and speakers on a wide variety of subjects.

Designed by Frank Lloyd Wright's Taliesin group of architects, the building gained its famous purple hue from Lloyd Wright's wife. She selected the color from the lining of a seashell.

Although the building was totally renovated in 2002, including the expansion of the stagehouse and the lobby areas, nary a ghost was to be found.

I questioned several docents as well as the hall's media relations personnel and even a manager or two.

"There are no ghosts here," they all said.

Or are they simply hiding somewhere in the cavernous hall?

Perhaps they are below the stage where the Steinways are stored, or in the top of the newly expanded stage house, or in one of the many staircases that lead up, down and around the building.

Should you attend a performance there, pay attention.

You may hear more than a good joke.

You might see more than a lovely ballet.

Hundreds of famous stars have played that stage. Many have passed on. There must certainly be some who would return for an encore in that unique building on the shore of Sarasota Bay. Perhaps the spirit of the building's architect, Frank Lloyd Wright will return to check on the recent work.

Equally elusive were the spirits of Marie Selby Botanical Gardens. Despite questions to several employees and volunteers at that lovely site, I could find no hint of any mysterious sounds save the gentle whistling in the bamboo groves and the sounds of the waves lapping the shore beneath the mangrove trees.

Should you discover one or more of these elusive spirits, please let me know at www.historicvenicepress.com.

I will be out and about, seeking more ghosts along the Gulf as my hunt for tales and legends continues.

About the author

Photo by Heidi Adams Coventry Cool

Kim Cool has written business, needlecraft and travel books. This is the second in a series of books about ghosts along the Gulf Coast. In *Ghost Stories of Venice*, she first explored the possibilities of West Florida spirits.

By day, the Sweet Briar College graduate writes about Venice, entertainment, homes and travel as the Features Editor of the *Venice Gondolier Sun*.. She is a member of the Venice Archives and Area Historical Collection, the Venice Historical Society, Historical Society of Sarasota County, the Advisory Board of the Salvation Army, a national synchronized, senior competition and gold test judge for the United States Figure Skating Association, a former competitive curler at the national level and a charter member of the Florida Curling Club.

The writer has won awards from the Florida Press Association for articles about the environment, religion and travel.

She is listed in Who's Who of American Women, Who's Who in the South and Southwest and other reference works.

Ackowledgments

This book would not have been written without the help of those who shared their stories and those who put me in touch with others who had stories to tell.

Nor would this book have been written without help from the spirits that were willing to make themselves known and the friends and colleagues who were willing to read the prepublication stories.

Others helped just by being there or, in some cases, by not being there so I could go haunting.

The ghosts:
Only the spirits know for sure who they are, or ... were.

The people:
Charles J. Adams III, Patty and Robert Atkins, Doug Bolduc, Shannon Brigham, Phillip Burkhart, Chris Burtless, Anne Cederberg, Pat and Trevor Charnley, Donna Des Isles, Rina Farlow, Richard Fischer, Rilla Fleming, Kelly Fores, Alison Guest, Vicky Hadley, Carol Harwood, Richard Hopkins, Pat Horwell, Gunther and Ilse Kern, DJ Kowal, Jeanne Lambert, Carol Lee, Ron Michael Marcello, McCarty, Roberta McDonald,Jerry McMullan, Kevin McQuaid, Bob and Melinda Mudge, Debbie and Rafael, Perez, Lynn and Rich Rosa, Dale Shields, Kyle Ennis Turoff, Vida Urbonas, Jenny Wallenda, Burton Wolfe

Bibliography

Adams, Charles J. "Cape May Ghost Stories, Book III." Exeter House Books. 2002.

Adams, Charles J. "New York City Ghost Stories." Exeter House Books. 1996.

Adams, Charles J. "Philadelphia Ghost Stories." Exeter House Books. 1998.

"An Historical Architectural Survey." Venice, Florida, second printing, 1995.

Blackman, W. Hayden. "The Field Guide to North American Hauntings." Three Rivers Press. 1998.

Buck, Pat Ringling; Corbino, Marcia; Dean, Kevin. "A History of Visual Art in Sarasota." University Press of Florida, 2003

Downer, Deborah. Editor. "Classic American Ghost Stories." August House Publishers. 1990.

Guiley, Rosemary Ellen. "Ghosts and Spirits," Second Edition. Checkmark Books. 2000.

Hauck, Dennis William. "The National Directory Haunted Places." Penquin Books, 1996.

Jones, Richard. "Haunted Britain and Ireland." Barnes & Noble Books. 2001

Matthew, Janet Snyder. "Venice, Journey From Horse and Chaise, a History of Venice, Florida." Pine Level Press Inc. 1989.

Bibliography

McSherry, Jr. Frank D.; Waugh, Charles G. Greenburg, Martin H.; editors. "Great American Ghost Stories." Rutledge Hill Press.1991.

Mendoza, Patrick M. "Between Midnight and Morning, Historic Hauntings and Ghost Tales." August House Publishers Inc. 2000.

Ogden, Tom. "The Complete Idiot's Guide to Ghosts and Hauntings." Alpha Books, a division on Macmillan USA, Inc. 1999.

Pitkin, David J. "Ghosts of the Northeast." Aurora Publications. 2002

Periodicals
Newsletter of the Historical Society of Sarasota County
Sarasota Herald Tribune
Sarasota Journal
Sarasota Magazine
The News (Sarasota)

HISTORIC VENICE PRESS
ORDER FORM

Ghost Stories of Sarasota...$12.95
      ISBN 0-9721655-1-7

Ghost Stories of Venice...$8.95
      ISBN 0-9721655-0-9

Indicate the number of books you wish to order below:

Number
ordered

_____   Sarasota @ 12.95   _____

_____   Venice @ 8.95   _____

           Sub total   _____

Florida residents add 7 percent sales tax   _____

Shipping to one address   _____ $3.50

TOTAL AMOUNT ENCLOSED: _____

MAIL TO:
Historic Venice Press
PO Box 800
Venice, FL 34285

177

Afterword

If you have a story to share about a paranormal experience anywhere along the Gulf Coast of Florida, please contact me by e-mail at:
www.historicvenicepress.com

or by regular mail to Kim Cool at:
Historic Venice Press
PO Box 800
Venice, FL 34285

I hope you enjoyed sharing my Sarasota adventure.

Kim Cool
Venice, Florida
June 2003